Becoming a Literacy Leader

Supporting Learning and Change

JENNIFER ALLEN

Foreword by Karen Szymusiak and Franki Sibberson

Stenhouse Publishers
Portland, Maine

Stenhouse Publishers
www.stenhouse.com

Library of Congress Cataloging-in-Publication Data
Allen, Jennifer, 1969–
    Becoming a literacy leader : supporting learning and change / Jennifer Allen.
        p. cm.
        Includes bibliographical references.
        ISBN 1-57110-419-4
        1. Language arts teachers—Training of—United States. 2. Literacy—Study and teaching—United States. 3. Literacy programs—United States. I. Title.
LB1576.A61285 2006
372.6—dc22   2005054111

Cover and interior design by Martha Drury
Cover illustration "Potentials" by Deborah DeWit Marchant

Manufactured in the United States of America on acid-free paper
17 16 15 14 13 12   12 11 10 9 8 7

Dedicated to my mom, Eileen Burk,
my lifelong coach

Contents

Foreword

Many of us recognize the power of literacy and the critical role of conversations with children in our classrooms. In this book, we are reminded that conversations and collaboration with colleagues are critical to teachers as well. We think about our literate lives as teachers in ways that make us stronger and smarter teachers of children. We study the experts and what they have to say about literacy development, and we reinvent our own strategies as learners and teachers. We embrace these new perspectives and mesh them into our teaching lives. Jennifer Allen values these conversations and collaborations, understanding teachers as learners. She shares with readers the intricate ways she is able to help teachers find their way in the complex world of teaching.

What struck us about Jen's vision of her job is her respect for teachers. Instead of seeing herself as the "literacy expert," Jen has become a colleague, sounding board, friend, and resource for the teachers in her elementary schools. She doesn't see her job as one in which she tells teachers the "right way" to do things. Instead, she realizes the challenges that teachers face and finds ways to support them as they figure out how best to meet the needs of their students.

Jen's book reminds us that in-depth thinking and study are important to learning. She doesn't fill her book with activities for teachers. Instead, she shares her story and the new understanding that she and her colleagues have gained while she's been the literacy specialist for her schools. She shares some of the specific issues that she and her staff have dealt with over time. As we read, we begin to understand how she balances her roles as listener, partner, and agent of change. She understands that teachers need opportunities to direct their own learning, and she is there to support them.

Jen's work is based on research, but she also understands what teachers face from her own experiences as a classroom teacher. She doesn't present a program that magically meets the needs of children and teachers. Instead, she shares her beliefs and passions about teachers and learners and the types of change that can happen with strong leadership. Although Jen's role is that of a literacy specialist, this book has huge implications for all school leaders—principals, literacy support personnel, central office administration, and staff developers.

This book honors the nature of teaching in many ways. Teaching has become a complex symphony of decisions and practices that challenge teachers to understand literacy and children in ways that have never been expected before. Teachers are knowledgeable about their craft and responsive to the many intricacies in the lives of children. They listen to children, watch them learn, and respond with the decisions and practices that they anticipate will move them toward independence as readers and writers. Teaching is sometimes demeaned in these days of accountability, but in this book we find hope and respect for teachers' dedication and expertise.

Imagine the challenges that face new teachers coming into the profession. They can be supported by the literacy specialists, like Jen, and the colleagues in their school who immerse them in the conversations about the literacy lives of children and the best practices that will support them. Experienced teachers can benefit from the work of a literacy specialist like Jen as well, because she understands that teaching and learning are always linked. Each year teachers welcome a new group of students with all their knowledge and skill. Day by day they reach out to students and learn from them. Jen's role becomes a journey of trust, walking alongside teachers as they teach and learn.

As a literacy specialist, Jen encourages teachers to slow down and reflect on their teaching. That often happens in a study group where teachers get together to talk about a professional book they have read. Sustaining a focus of study over time encourages teachers to develop new understandings in ways that are meaningful and purposeful. Jen helps teachers explore what experts have to offer while retaining their own individuality, responding to the needs of the children in their classes.

And so Jen's journey is an awakening. She defines her role as literacy specialist by what she has learned from working with talented and dedicated teachers. She understands that teachers never stop learning, and that she can support their attempts to develop new skills and expertise. Her work as a literacy leader melds collaboration and conversation, as teachers find their way toward new understandings and insights. Together they come to recognize the power of literacy and the energy of shared learning.

Karen Szymusiak and Franki Sibberson, authors of *Still Learning to Read*

Acknowledgments

"Finding the extraordinary in ordinary moments."
<small>Anonymous</small>

It still feels funny to have written a book "solo" since the product is a reflection of my work and interactions with so many individuals and educators. I have been fortunate to be surrounded by so many amazing people who continue to inspire my thinking.

Brenda Power, you are a visionary writer and editor. You have the gift for finding diamonds in the rough and making them sparkle. I am forever grateful for your insights, wisdom, and friendship over the last twelve years.

Philippa Stratton, thanks for taking me along for the ride as you explored and created *Read, Share, and Teach*. Your faith in my work has fueled my love for professional development.

Jay Kilburn, thank you for shepherding the book through production. Martha Drury, thank you for making it so beautiful.

Carolyn and Lesley, you are extraordinary teachers. Thanks for reading drafts, talking me through my ideas, and providing honest feedback. You have pushed my learning to new frontiers. I am honored to collaborate with you in your classrooms.

Rose, you are the "we" in the I. Thanks for teaching me early literacy. You are the perfect partner.

I am fortunate to work with visionary leaders and administrators. You have supported me even when I haven't followed the "popular" path. Allan Martin, Harriet Trafford, Joe Mattos, and Eric Haley, you are gifted leaders who have helped guide me in my journey as a literacy leader. Thanks for letting me find my own way.

I am indebted to my colleagues at the George J. Mitchell School, who started out with me in the teacher research group more than eight years ago. The experience introduced me to the world of study groups. Thanks for satisfying my thirst for new learning.

Thanks to all the teachers, Title I support staff, and students at the George J. Mitchell School and the Albert S. Hall School. I thank you for patience, honesty, and support in helping me learn on my journey as a literacy leader. Without you there would be no book.

I would like to thank Louise McCannell for coaching me as a new teacher and years later mentoring me again as I took my first steps as a literacy specialist.

Franki Sibberson, thanks for asking me when I was planning to write my own book. Your interest in "My Life in Seven Stories" was the subtle nudge of encouragement that I needed to take the next step. Thanks also to Karen Szymusiak for your thoughtful words in the foreword.

Jill Reinhart, Carol Franz, and Colleen Buddy, thanks for your early reviews and insights on the proposal that helped shape my writing.

Ralph Fletcher and Georgia Heard, thanks for your work in the field of writing. Your thinking has inspired my work with teachers.

Thanks to Leslie Lloyd, Cathy Lovendahl, Melissa Miller, Jill Michaud, and Jeni Frazee for letting me share your stories.

A special wave from the heart to Righteous Red.

Todd, Ben, and Sam, you are my seven stories. Thanks for all your time and support. Without your help, this book would not have been!

CHAPTER ONE

Introduction

This is not work for the faint-hearted. To do it well requires a calm disposition and the trust-building skills of a mediator combined with the steely determination and perseverance of an innovator.

ELLEN GUINEY

I Am

Who am I? What am I? I have read all of the definitions of reading coach, literacy specialist, and reading apprentice. I am reluctant to define myself as anything but a teacher. What I can do is tell you about myself, and share my stories about becoming a literacy leader.

I am fast talking, fast walking, and full of life. I spring out of bed each morning ready to tackle new challenges, and flop into bed at night depleted of all energy. My mind is always at work, churning with new ideas and thinking. I am a listener, a partner, and a subtle agent for change. I work with teachers, Title I reading technicians, parents, literacy specialists, administrators, and students. My work is multilayered. It begins at the district level as a member of the leadership team, collecting and analyzing data to determine district needs, plan initiatives, and set goals. From here it moves to the school level, where my responsibilities branch out in many directions: Title I coordinator, staff developer, and developer of curriculum and assessment.

The layers of my role move into the classroom, where I work with teachers and students. I support school initiatives by providing professional development for all staff. I provide opportunities for teachers to pursue new learning through participation in study groups.

I have worked as a licensed literacy specialist for grades 3 through 5 since 2000. Before that I taught third grade for nine years. I entered my current position as literacy specialist without a job description. The district had redirected their focus on literacy for grades K–5 because the results of state testing indicated that our students were struggling to *meet the standard* in reading and writing. I was hired to "support literacy." There had not been a literacy specialist in my position for eight years. I have had the luxury of creating my identity as a literacy support person and establishing a partnership with the K–2 literacy specialist. My identity as a literacy leader has developed and evolved over the last five years.

We Are

We are a K–12 school district. We have four large schools. The George J. Mitchell School serves students in kindergarten through grade 3. There are approximately thirty classroom teachers and six hundred students, plus support staff. Students then move to the Albert S. Hall School, which serves students in grades 4 and 5. This school has roughly twenty teachers and three hundred students. After fifth grade, students move to the junior high school for grades 6 through 8 and then to the high school for grades 9 through 12. I work at the George J. Mitchell School (focusing on grade 3 teachers and students) and also at the Albert S. Hall School (grades 4 and 5).

The school district is in a small city in Maine. The free and reduced-price lunch population is about 56 percent, and we have a yearly transient rate of 33 percent. By tracking students over a three-year period we have found that our transient rate increases to more than 50 percent. Students come and go and come back. In this same town we have two private colleges that employ many professors. We are a hub for a regional hospital that employs medical staff. The children of these well-educated professionals are thrown into the mix of our struggling community—a community that once housed prosperous paper mills.

Shared Literacy Leadership

It feels awkward to write this book using the word *I*. I find myself typing the word *we* only to delete it and replace it with *I*. I am part of a team and it is through this shared leadership team that I support literacy. I collaborate with principals, literacy specialists, teachers, librarians, support staff, and parents. We work together to achieve goals that we have set as a district.

My journey as a literacy specialist includes my partner Rose Patterson, the K–2 literacy specialist. Although the stories I share reflect my personal experiences in becoming a literacy leader, my overall literacy journey includes collaborating with Rose since 2000. We work together generating new ideas, processing new learning, and ensuring that the literacy curriculum and student learning is streamlined for students in kindergarten through grade 5. We work to ensure consistency between grade levels, and across buildings within the district.

My work as literacy specialist in supporting professional development within the district is multilayered. I work at the school level to provide professional development at monthly staff meetings to all teachers, creating a common understanding of best literacy practices. I facilitate teacher study groups so that teachers' individual professional needs are met. In addition, I work with teachers and students in classrooms, supporting teachers as they implement new teaching strategies.

The district is committed to providing high-quality in-house professional development. The focus is on providing professional development to increase the quality of instruction that is delivered to students. By working in-house supporting teachers in literacy, I am able to respond to teachers' needs and provide modeling and follow-through support. Literacy support is delivered in the natural setting of the classrooms in which the teachers work. Professional development opportunities within the district have been designed to meet the standards put forth by the U.S. Department of Education and the National Staff Development Council (online at www.nsdc.org/standards/index.cfm) and incorporate the latest research on providing high-quality professional development. The position of literacy specialist as reading coach supports these standards for providing in-house professional development opportunities.

My Stories

One of the greatest challenges has been learning to balance the demands of the job. Because the role of literacy specialist as reading coach is relatively new, I have traveled an interesting road in defining and shaping my role as a literacy coach.

This book is a reflection of my journey to becoming a literacy leader. They are my stories, the moments that have guided my own learning. It is my hope that by sharing my stories, others will be inspired to continue and persevere through their own journeys of becoming literacy leaders.

CHAPTER TWO

A Room of One's Own for Literacy

The teaching profession has never been honored with any first-class touches. But a quiet room used for staff development can become truly elegant when it contains a tray of cookies, a basket of fresh fruit, a pot of good coffee with real milk. It can be made elegant with the addition of carefully duplicated articles, well-thought-out calendars, and invitations to attend relevant conferences.

SHELLEY HARWAYNE, IN GOING PUBLIC

I vividly remember walking for the first time into the classroom I was assigned as a literacy specialist. I anxiously unlocked the door of the room in the basement. There I stood, staring at a large bare space, empty except for a mound of dusty old literacy materials in a three-foot-high pile in the center of the floor.

My only request as I moved from the position of third-grade teacher to literacy specialist was to be given a classroom. I knew that much of my time would be spent helping teachers in the school understand and implement best practices in literacy. When I imagined what I wanted the room to be like, I dreamed of an inviting space like the ones designed for children by so many classroom teachers I admired—colorful, bright, clean, and inviting.

There was a reason why the room was bare and the materials were dusty. There had not been a literacy specialist in the school for eight years. Teachers in the school had a history of literature-based reading instruction long before other districts had replaced basal readers. The school had a wide selection of multiple copies of children's literature texts that were housed in closets in the hallway outside my newly designated literacy room. My new school had a veteran staff, and I often heard parents say, "We don't have to worry about our kids at the Hall School. The teachers are excellent and know the kids."

I was young enough to be the daughter of many of the teachers. I knew that the staff was knowledgeable and didn't want or need an outsider telling them the "right way" to teach reading and writing. What they needed was support to meet the ever-changing demands of state and national mandates. I predicted that my expertise and energy would be best used if they came to see me as an invaluable resource. The design and materials of the literacy room would be at the center of my becoming that resource for colleagues. I thought hard not only about the layout of the room, but about how I wanted teachers to use it, interacting with each other and me. I hung up new white sheer curtains, plugged in two lamps for soft lighting, positioned framed student artwork on the walls, and set out to create the literacy room.

When I began to plan how I would use the space, I considered how the layout and displays might inspire teachers. Third-grade teacher Joanne Hindley in her book *In the Company of Children* quotes her colleague Isobel Beaton in describing the "geography" of a space:

> *Geography is everything. I realized that I needed to figure out what I wanted to happen and how my classroom geography could support and enhance or inhibit or deter those goals. A country's geography predetermines a lot of what goes on in that country— for example, rivers and mountains form natural barriers and then people/society put up others; a railroad cut, a highway, a wall. But in my classroom I determine the geography. I can put up barriers to communication or I can set things up to encourage conversation. I can establish lonely islands of I's or I can form communities and provinces of we's. Everyone can have his or her own of each thing or groups can share. I can make that sharing difficult or I can support it. All the energy in my room can come from me or I can*

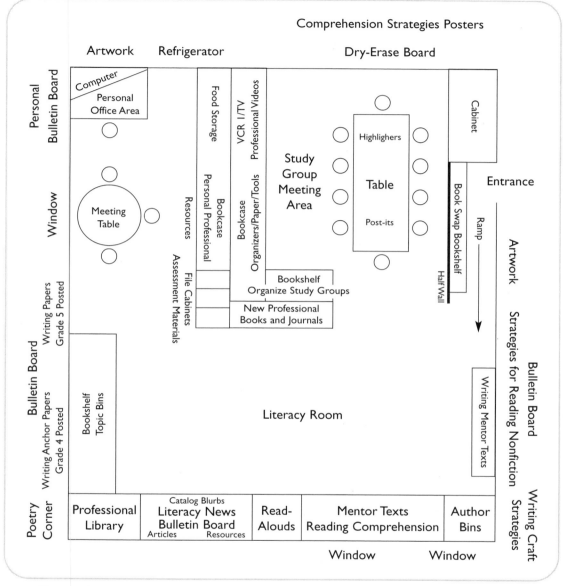

Figure 2.1
Blueprint of
Literacy Room
Design

have constellations of energy. And the geography I put in place will do that for me. (1996, p. 5)

I needed to establish a geography in the room where even the busiest teacher would feel the urge to pause and check out a new professional article. With all the rushed feeling of trying to do too much in too little time in schools, I wanted to create a haven where teachers felt comfortable lingering over new children's books. Teachers needed a place where a chance encounter with a colleague to discuss a difficult student could be extended over a cup of coffee and some browsing among current journals. The physical environment would set the tone of respect, and it needed to encourage collaboration, too.

A space can be inviting and still rigorous, as Debbie Miller writes in *Reading with Meaning*:

> *Rigorous environments do not have to be rigid or restrictive. I know we have mandates, time lines, and important tests to give. And still I say slow down! Learning to read should be a joyful experience. . . . Let them know when they say or do something smart; give them credit and ask them to share. Help children access what they already know and figure out how to help them make connections to something new. Be geniune. Laugh. Love. Be patient. You're creating a community of readers and thinkers; you're building relationships and establishing trust. Come October, you'll be glad you did. (2002, p. 26)*

If kids thrive in rooms that are literate, warm, and organized, surely teachers would, too. Lots of materials available for teachers are delightful to read; discussing them with colleagues can help anyone slow down and get the joy back in their teaching.

I spent my first day looking through those old reading materials in the center of the room (materials that no one had used in the eight years since the school had had a literacy specialist on staff). I couldn't imagine hooking teachers into new learning with outdated workbook manuals, molding professional books, or black-and-white comprehension games. I did something unthinkable for a teacher: I pulled out black garbage bags from the custodian's supply cabinet and bagged up virtually everything in that pile.

The custodian was a tremendous resource, far beyond hauling all those old materials to the Dumpster. He also spent time giving me a school tour, helping me find furniture for my space. He uncovered a wooden desk, a large meeting table, chairs, file cabinets, and old bookshelves for my literacy classroom. He was ever-so-patient, bringing me to the various storage areas hidden around the school. At this point, I had furniture and was able to set up the physical framework for the room.

Wall Space

At first glance, my room looks like a classroom for students. It is only through a closer examination that anyone would realize it is a room designed primarily for teachers.

The walls are an important way to build a community within the literacy room, introducing literacy strategies and providing information about best practices. Ideas and strategies are posted over time. I provide visual resources for ideas and concepts that we are exploring as a school. Many of the items posted on the walls are in response to conversations I have with teachers. Displays include the following:

- Student anchor papers that demonstrate state standards in writing
- Reading comprehension strategies
- Elements of writing
- Ideas for initiating book discussions
- Reading strategies

My display of strategies for reading nonfiction includes text features, how to mark thinking in text, graphic organizers, and applications of a research strategy from a recent issue of *The Reading Teacher.*

For example, one of the bulletin boards currently has a layout of Nonfiction Reading Strategies with models of nonfiction access features and completed graphic organizers. Copies of articles and ideas are available in folders stapled to the board so that teachers can take these quick ideas with them.

These articles are currently available for teachers to take:

Stein, D., and P. Beed. 2004. "Bridging the gap between fiction and nonfiction in the literature circle setting." *The Reading Teacher* 57, 510–518.

Yopp, R., and H. Yopp. 2004. "Preview-predict-confirm: thinking about the language and content of informational text." *The Reading Teacher* 58, 79–82.

Giard, M. 2001. "Lesson Ideas to Help Students Successfully Read Nonfiction Texts." STAR Reading Assessment Training.

Literacy News Bulletin Board

The literacy news bulletin board is devoted to professional resources. It contains information such as fall and spring literacy assessment expectations, book lists, articles, conference opportunities, and new professional book titles. I use two-pocket folders cut in half and stapled to the bulletin board to house the articles for teachers. I work hard to be up to date on the latest read–aloud and picture books. I created a list of my hot new picks for teachers to aid in their book buying. These lists are also on this board. I've continued this practice and update my lists every fall and spring. I am constantly on the lookout for new literacy resources. Because I am current on available resources and new publications, it doesn't take a lot of time to stay up to date. It is a continual process of sifting and skimming through catalogs and advertisements for new purchases. I am always looking for resources that will meet teachers' needs.

Another strategy I use for generating interest in new professional materials is to cut the blurbs on new professional publications out of the color catalogs and post them on the literacy news board. Publishers usually provide the table of contents for their books and the grade levels they are targeting. My hope is that teachers will become more aware of the array of resources that are available to them.

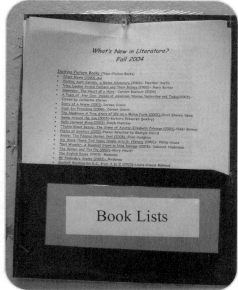

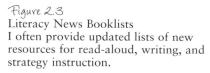

Figure 2.2
Literacy News Bulletin Board
The literacy news bulletin board includes handouts already copied for teachers of latest resources, lists of award-winning books, recent news articles, scanned covers of new books, and catalog descriptions from publishers of videos and books that might interest the staff.

Figure 2.3
Literacy News Booklists
I often provide updated lists of new resources for read-aloud, writing, and strategy instruction.

Library of Mentor Texts

As a third-grade teacher, my classroom library consisted of various bins of organized books. The books were accessible, organized, and visually appealing. I wanted to create a model classroom library of kids' books that teachers could use as a resource. Because I was on a limited budget that first year, I bought bins at a local dollar store in which to organize my books.

I couldn't immediately create a full library of books for teaching reading and writing, so I decided to focus on "mentor texts" that first year. I collected hardcover picture books that could be used as mentor texts to teach the craft of writing and to teach reading comprehension strategies. I used *Craft Lessons* by Ralph Fletcher and JoAnn Portalupi to get started. I labeled the outside of the book bins each with different elements of writing craft:

- Leads
- Character
- Story Structures
- Setting
- Endings
- Titles
- Voice
- Word Choice
- Language

Here is an example of the books in the Characters bin (see Figure 2.4). The first column lists the books I used when I first developed the bin; the second column consists of books added over the years.

Figure 2.4

BOOKS IN CHARACTER BIN

Mentor Texts for Crafting "Characters" (Recommended in *Craft Lessons*)	Mentor Texts Added Over the Last Few Years
Fig Pudding, Ralph Fletcher	*When Marian Sang*, Pam Muñoz Ryan
Sarah, Plain and Tall, Patricia MacLachlan	*Grandpa Never Lies*, Ralph Fletcher
The Stories Julian Tells, Ann Cameron	*Hey, Little Ant*, Phillip Hoose
Tar Beach, Faith Ringgold	*Insects Are My Life*, Megan McDonald
Honey I Love, Eloise Greenfield	*When I Was Your Age: Original Stories about Growing Up*, Edited by Amy Ehrlich
The Great Gilly Hopkins, Katherine Patterson	
Wilma Unlimited, Kathleen Krull	*Gandhi*, Demi
Yolanda's Genius, Carol Fenner	*Rosebud and Red Flannel*, Ethel Pochocki
Teammates, Peter Golenbock	*The Sweetest Fig*, Chris Van Allsburg
Amelia and Eleanor Go for a Ride, Pam Muñoz Ryan	*Just a Dream*, Chris Van Allsburg
	Eleanor, Barbara Cooney
Chester's Way, Kevin Henkes	*Sophie's Masterpiece*, Eileen Spinelli
Mufaro's Beautiful Daughters, John Steptoe	*The Race*, Caroline Repchuk
Miss Rumphius, Barbara Cooney	*Olivia*, Ian Falconer
My Great-Aunt Arizona, Gloria Houston	*The Spider and the Fly*, Tony DiTerlizzi
	Miss Viola and Uncle Ed Lee, Alice Faye Duncan
	Albert, Donna Jo Napoli
	Superdog: The Heart of a Hero, Caralyn Buehner
	Amber Was Brave, Essie Was Smart, Vera B. Williams
	Ida B . . . and Her Plans to Maximize Fun, Avoid Disaster, and (Possibly) Save the World, Katherine Hannigan
	What Would Joey Do?, Jack Gantos

Figure 2.5
Sample Writing
Craft Bins of
Mentor Texts

For examples of other writing craft bins developed over time, please
see the appendix.

I organized another section of the room with a bookcase filled with
plastic bins of picture books to teach reading comprehension strategies.
The text our teaching staff used at the time was *Strategies That Work* by
Stephanie Harvey and Anne Goudvis. It was a logical next step to provide
teachers with resources that were cited in the book they were reading.
Mentor texts bins for reading comprehension were divided into these categories:

- Making Connections
- Visualizing
- Asking Questions
- Determining Important Information
- Making Inferences
- Synthesizing

I made the lists available to teachers in a common folder on the school
server so they would be aware of the bins of new materials in the room. It
wasn't long before teachers started coming to the room to borrow entire
bins for their classrooms.

New bins have been developed over the years to reflect projects that
are happening in classrooms and new curriculum mandates. Author and
topic bins develop as I respond to teachers' needs. For example, an alter-

EXAMPLE OF BOOKS IN "MAKING CONNECTIONS" BIN

Mentor Texts for "Making Connections" (From *Strategies That Work*)	Mentor Texts Added to the "Making Connections" Bin Over the Last Few Years
Hey World, Here I Am, Jean Little	*Lilly's Purple Plastic Purse,* Kevin Henkes
Wilfrid Gordon McDonald Partridge, Mem Fox	*Miss Alaineus: A Vocabulary Disaster,* Debra Frasier
Julius the Baby of the World, Kevin Henkes	*Fig Pudding,* Ralph Fletcher
Shelia Ray the Brave, Kevin Henkes	*Grandpa Never Lies,* Ralph Fletcher
My Rotten Red-Headed Older Brother, Patricia Polacco	*When Sophie Gets Really Really Angry,* Molly Bang
	Some Things Are Scary, Florence Parry Heide
Some Birthday!, Patricia Polacco	*Baseball, Snakes, and Summer Squash: Poems About Growing Up,* Donald Graves
Thank You, Mr. Falker, Patricia Polacco	
Fly Away Home, Eve Bunting	*School Picture Day,* Lynn Plourde
Alexander and the Terrible, Horrible, No Good Very Bad Day, Judith Viorst	*Super-Completely and Totally the Messiest,* Judith Viorst
The Relatives Came, Cynthia Rylant	*What Are You So Grumpy About?,* Tom Lichtenheld
Birthday Presents, Cynthia Rylant	*Bedhead,* Margie Palatini
	Roxaboxen, Barbara Cooney
	When Lightning Comes in a Jar, Patricia Polacco
	The Graves Family, Patricia Polacco
	Slithery Jake, Rose Marie Provencher
	Wemberly Worried, Kevin Henkes
	The English Roses, Madonna
	Olivia, Ian Falconer
	It's Disgusting and We Ate It!, James Solheim
	Hey, Daddy! Animal Fathers and Their Babies, Mary Batten
	Visiting Aunt Sylvia's: A Maine Adventure, Heather Austin
	Sweet Tooth, Margie Palatini

Figure 2.6

native education teacher was trying to hook her reluctant readers with the captivating subject of the sinking of the *Titanic*. I searched to find resources at different reading levels so we could introduce the topic and layer the resources for student learning. Together we created a bin of new resources.

Ideas for author tubs at intermediate grades:

- Chris Van Allsburg, Picture books to teach comprehension strategies
- Cynthia Rylant, Author to study craft of writing
- Eve Bunting, Picture books to teach theme
- Patricia Polacco, Picture books to teach comprehension strategies
- Jean Craighead George, Grade 5 author study
- Andrew Clements, Grade 4 author study
- Sharon Creech, Great author study
- Gary Paulsen, Great author study

Ideas for resource bins:

- Environment
- *Titanic*
- Maine Studies
- Holidays
- Persuasion
- Point of View
- Bullying
- Friendship
- Famous People
- Where in the World?
- Math Resources
- Make Something
- Kid Picks
- Nonfiction Picks

In this bin, teachers can find resources on the *Titanic*.

The first year was just a beginning. I continue to purchase new books and add to the bins annually. I am always on the lookout for new picture books that can be added to the mentor texts bins. These bins are heavily used by teachers. Teachers come to the room daily looking for specific books or sometimes just to browse through the bins for new ideas.

Professional Library

I also have a bookcase for professional books and journals. I sift through material to find the best new publications so that the staff has the best resources available to them. I skim journals, catalogs, and flyers sent through the mail almost daily.

If a teacher reads a book and is really excited about digging deeper and trying out some of the strategies presented, I usually tell them to keep the book. If a teacher really wants to try new ideas from a book, it's important that they have easy access to that resource, and they shouldn't have to worry about returning it. I will then simply buy another copy for the professional bookcase. I keep an updated list of professional books in a database in a common folder on the school server so that teachers are aware of the professional books available within the school. Many teachers borrow professional books for summer reading. I also purchased school memberships to the International Reading Association and the National Council for Teachers of English so that teachers would have access to professional journals.

Read–Aloud Corner

I have a small bookshelf for new read-alouds. I am continually looking for new chapter books that could be read-aloud favorites in classrooms. Once a month I spend a weekday afternoon at Barnes and Noble scouring their shelves and reading excerpts from books. Teachers come to the literacy room often to look for a new read-aloud and hear what I would recommend. Reading the books myself helps make my recommendations more credible.

My all-time favorite read-aloud picks include the following:

- *Because of Winn-Dixie*, Kate DiCamillo
- *Lost on a Mountain in Maine*, Donn Fendler
- *Fig Pudding*, Ralph Fletcher
- *Flying Solo*, Ralph Fletcher
- *No More Dead Dogs*, Gordon Korman
- *What Would Joey Do?*, Jack Gantos
- *Pictures of Hollis Woods*, Patricia Reilly Giff
- *Baseball, Snakes, and Summer Squash: Poems About Growing Up*, Donald Graves
- *Ida B . . . and Her Plans to Maximize Fun, Avoid Disaster, and (Possibly) Save the World*, Katherine Hannigan
- *Aquamarine*, Alice Hoffman
- *Arthur for the Very First Time*, Patricia MacLachlan

To find new read-alouds, I go to these places:

- *Book Links* magazine
- *Library Journal*
- Annual Children's Book Choices (IRA)
- Annual Teacher Choices (IRA)
- Newbery and Newbery Honor Selections
- Book Publishers at Conferences

I do not have a sign-out system for borrowing materials from the literacy room. I encourage teachers to take materials freely and return books when they are finished using them. If a book turns up missing, I simply purchase a replacement text. I do not want to put my energy into hounding teachers to return resources—the very resources that I want them to feel comfortable borrowing and using to change their teaching.

Study Group Meeting Area

I knew I would use the literacy room for teacher study groups, so I designated a corner to serve as a group meeting place. Too often teacher study groups meet in temporary space—tables or desks hastily shoved together, in a corner of the cafeteria or school library, with teachers hunched over in chairs designed for much younger bodies. I wanted to create a space that would always be there for teachers, even when study groups were not meeting. The permanence of the space emphasizes its importance for our staff.

The nine-foot-long table comfortably fits eight to nine chairs. There is a dry-erase board that is convenient for groups to use. The table always has a basket of tools for noting resources or interesting ideas in texts, stocked with supplies such as highlighters, pens, pencils, Post-its, and Post-it flags.

Food is also essential to have on hand. Teachers rush in before students in the morning for resources, or the literacy room is often their last stop at the end of a tiring day. I got a small refrigerator using bonus points from book club purchases. I always stock the refrigerator with water and soda, and a basket with candy. Teachers know they are welcome to help themselves and make themselves at home while working in the room.

During the second year I developed a library of professional videos. These videos are shelved in the study group meeting area. I collected book club bonus points to buy a television and video player for the space. We

Materials for marking text are on the table, the videos are available for viewing, and a small refrigerator is stocked with refreshments.

often view video segments during study groups, and I didn't want to waste time finding equipment, setting it up, and breaking it down after each meeting.

The other justification for having this equipment permanently in the room is that I want teachers to be able to use this space and revisit videos during their leisure. Teachers often come to the study group area during a lunch break to review a segment of video.

Staff Picks

I am often asked what I am reading. Many teachers know I keep a journal of the recent titles I have read and ask to take a look for book ideas. Nothing thrills me more than talking with another person about a new book. It was because of my personal passion for reading that I jumped at the recommendation of creating a staff swap of adult books.

This idea started small. I took $250 from a grant and went with a few Title I teachers to a local bookstore and purchased books in various genres. It was fun to buy books that we thought others on the staff would enjoy.

Here are some favorite staff picks:

- *The Secret Life of Bees*, Sue Monk Kidd
- *Running with Scissors*, Augusten Burroughs
- *The Lobster Chronicles*, Linda Greenlaw
- *Memories of a Geisha*, Arthur Golden
- *What We Keep*, Elizabeth Berg
- *The Da Vinci Code*, Dan Brown
- *Into the Wild*, Jon Krakauer
- *Blessings*, Anna Quindlen
- *Walk in the Woods*, Bill Bryson
- *Comfort Me with Apples*, Ruth Reichl
- *Three Junes*, Julia Glass

I organized the books in a couple of plastic bins and hung up a poster board with markers so that people could jot down thoughts on the books that they enjoyed. One of the Title I teachers also started posting the *New York Times* Best Sellers list. We ask that teachers just return the books when they finish reading them. Teachers who add their own books to the bins put their names in the books so that they can get the books back eventually. I am amazed at the number of teachers who borrow books, and who also bring their own books to the room to lend.

Teachers are free to borrow books from the bin of staff picks.

Community Resources

I have three file cabinets that contain additional resources for teachers. The first cabinet contains folders on books and author information. If teachers work with a book and have a new idea, they may make a copy and place it in the folder. The folders contain questions, graphic organizers, and reading strategies that teachers think worked with the book. New teachers often browse the folders for new book ideas, especially if they are working with the book for the first time.

The second file cabinet is devoted to resources related to reading, writing, and assessment. The files contain instructional strategies that teachers could try with students in the classroom. There are graphic organizers that can be used to support instruction. Most of the resources in these files come from the teachers themselves. I encourage teachers to share their ideas and organizers so that others can use them and tweak them to meet their individual needs.

Examples of topic folders in the file cabinet:

- Reading Comprehension
- Vocabulary Development
- Oral Reading Fluency
- Decoding Strategies
- High-Frequency Word Lists
- Nonfiction Access Features
- Craft Lessons for Writing
- Snapshot Writing
- Journal Writing
- Revision Strategies
- Editing Checklists

The last file cabinet stores forms used with the Developmental Reading Assessment. I keep the cabinet stocked with assessment materials so that teachers don't have to spend their time copying their own assessment forms. Teachers can pull forms from the cabinet and keep their kits stocked.

Personal Office Area

A corner of the room is reserved for my personal work area. I have a desk, computer, small round table, table lamp, and CD player. The area is often used for informal chats with colleagues. It is also an appropriate space to assess students one on one. I chose to have my work space in the room so that I would be visible and accessible. I am always available in the mornings and after school. Just being there when a teacher comes in to look for a resource is often enough to spark a discussion. I also help teachers find the resources they are looking for or direct them to new ones.

Book Swap

Although the literacy room was created for teachers, there is a small space designated solely for students. At the entrance of the room is a bookshelf of book bins filled with new books. These books are for a student book swap. Approximately 56 percent of our students receive free or reduced-price lunch. Many of our students do not have their daily basic needs for food and shelter met, let alone the need for a steady diet of books.

I often assess new students entering the district. My icebreaker questions are "Do you like reading?" and "What book are you reading at home right now?" When I started asking these questions, I was amazed at the number of children who told me they didn't like reading and didn't have any books at home. If they did have books, they were outdated or inappropriate for their reading ability. Studies by Stephen Krashen show that "Access to books from any source (home, school, public library) will be

The book-swap program for students has been extended to the entire school.

extremely helpful, and may guarantee the establishment of a reading habit. Often those who hate to read simply do not have access to books" (2004, p. 21). I wanted to get appropriate, appealing, and interesting books in the hands of kids.

I found myself back at the dollar store buying more plastic bins. This time the bins were to start a book-swap library for students. I spent $1,000 of federal grant money to start the project and filled the bins with inexpensive, high-interest books purchased through book clubs. I was deliberate in my selections. I purchased popular series, kid-grabbing books for the library. I also bought nonfiction, animal, sport, and how-to books to try to hook into the interests of even the most reluctant readers. I wanted kids to select books that they could actually read and were interested in reading. My mission was to get good books in the hands of kids—and lots of them.

I started the project by focusing on students who received Title I services, because these students needed extra support in the area of reading. Many of these kids also came from economically disadvantaged homes. We kicked off the book swap by having the students take a book of their choice. The deal was that whenever they finished the book or wanted a new one, all they had to do was come back any morning between 8:15 and 8:30 and swap the book for a new one. The students couldn't believe that we were giving them books to keep and that they never had to return them. It was interesting to see kids test the system and come back daily for a shiny new book! New students entering the district were also impressed that they could select any book they wanted and keep it. Because we wanted lots of books in the hands of kids, we decided to let the students select a book each trimester to keep. Students receiving Title I services were given three books a year to add to their home reading library. Students could always swap the books that we gave them with books in the book-swap bins.

Extending the Book Swap to the Entire School

On the third year of the project, one of the reading teachers who worked in the Title I program asked if this was something we could do for the whole school since there are many kids who can read but don't have access to books at home. I agreed that we had many students who would benefit from the book-swap program. Students have a daily home reading requirement, and yet do not always have access to books for the required projects. With a little extra money ($600 for a school of three hundred students), we extended the book swap to the whole school. We kicked off the swap by having every student in the school select a book. All students started with a book that they could trade. The teachers who work in the Title I program purchase the books now and maintain the bins because they are the ones working most closely with the students. On any given morning there are students in the literacy room returning books and searching for new ones to bring home and read. I am able to get an informal sense daily of what books are exciting kids, and how and why they are choosing them, and I use this information to help teachers match kids with books. It's great for the kids to look beyond their shelves of book-swap books to see that all their teachers are still learners and readers, too.

The literacy room has continued to evolve over the past several years. It all started with few resources and a limited budget. Many of the ideas in the room come from the teachers in the school, and teachers used it throughout the day. It is not uncommon to have at least five teachers stopping by the room on a given morning looking for different resources. The literacy room has fulfilled my vision for the literate, organized, purposeful, and accessible room that I brought with me that first day when all I had was an empty classroom with a mound of old reading materials, piled high in the middle of the floor.

CHAPTER THREE

"My Life in Seven Stories": A Model for a Required In-Service Program

Learning stamps you with its moments. . . . It isn't steady.

It's a pulse.

EUDORA WELTY, ONE WRITER'S BEGINNINGS

If you had only seven stories to tell of your life, what would they be? How would these stories reflect who you are as a person? Would one of your stories be the birth of your first child, or would it be a simple moment like hiking alone through the woods? Why?

These questions were the starting point for integrating professional development into required staff meetings. Part of my job is to find ways to provide brief training sessions within these regularly scheduled meetings, and it has proven to be one of the most challenging aspects of my work. In retrospect, success came only because I was willing to learn from repeated failed attempts to do something meaningful in these meetings.

When I started in this position as literacy specialist, staff meetings consisted of a traditional format where the principal went through an agenda of business items and staff listened and offered their input into scheduling and upcoming events. This was a comfortable and accepted format. Midway through my first year we had a change in administration, and a new principal joined the school. She had a vision for ongoing professional development, and saw staff meetings as a vehicle by which to fulfill that goal. She was committed to shifting away from the traditional staff meeting format to more of a forum for professional conversations.

We needed time to talk as a staff about writing, and it seemed that the meetings could provide the perfect forum for short jolts of learning new strategies for teaching it. Our local and state data indicated that writing was an area of continued weakness.

As we shifted to the new model, we still held on to a traditional staff meeting format. The first thirty minutes of the meeting followed a business agenda, and the last fifteen minutes were dedicated to conversations about writing instruction.

I vividly recall the first few meetings. Teachers were engaged, and participated during the business part. They were enthusiastic about discussing topics such as a code-red school-evacuation procedure. They would easily question, agree with, or challenge each other's thinking about the precise placement of playground equipment.

The whole tone of the meeting changed as we moved into our professional conversations. This portion of the staff meeting was intended to be a relaxed and risk-free opportunity to share our thinking about writing. I had chosen *The Writing Workshop* (Ray 2001) as our staff text. I had shared several texts with teachers, and this was the one they were most interested in exploring. I had even purchased beautiful new journals from Barnes & Noble for their writer's notebooks. I naively thought that everyone would welcome the opportunity to talk about writing, jumping into this new forum for learning with the same enthusiasm that they had had for discussing the new playground.

For the first session, teachers had been asked to read the introductory chapter of the book beforehand. I began by throwing out a question to prompt a discussion. The silence was deadly. I was the only one willing to share my thoughts on the reading, and the only one who put forth any personal writing. The only comment I heard was an exclamation about how much I must have spent on the journals. I didn't even have the energy to share that I had written a grant to purchase their writer's notebooks!

The rest of the year and the next two years were pretty much the same. The books and videos on writing changed, but little changed in the way of writing instruction in the school or the forced professional dialog during staff meetings. I continued to lead the group through awkward discussions, as teachers mumbled to one another, asking what chapter we were to have read.

I should not have been surprised at the passive nature of the staff. Research clearly indicates that teachers are more likely to resist professional development when it is imposed upon them (Sweeney 2003). Needless to say, I was anxiously awaiting new assessment data that might shift our professional development focus to math. I thought I was failing miserably as a literacy leader.

A New Start

Every summer the leadership team goes on a two-day retreat to analyze local and state data and set district goals for the year. The team consists of teachers, administrators, parents, community members, and, of course, literacy specialists. Once again, all of the assessment data indicated that we needed to improve drastically in writing. My hope that we would redirect to a math focus wasn't coming to pass.

We sat around a rectangular table as the leadership team began to write the school goals for the upcoming year. I was in a daze. I heard that the goal once again would be to increase student achievement in writing. My stomach tightened. I knew what was coming next. Our first activity under the goal would be to pursue professional development in the area of writing through our monthly staff meetings.

I had read all the research on leading effective change and knew that long-lasting change needed to occur from within our learning community. Yet it was still mighty tempting to call in an outside one-shot expert (Fullan 1991). I even went as far as to make a contact to bring in an outside expert on writing so that he could enlighten us with new knowledge. But my principal promised me that things would be different this year. She promised this year to dedicate the entire staff meeting to professional development. All I could think was that I would have even more awkward silence with a staff that wanted to go back to traditional meetings where we discussed playground equipment. Instead of fifteen minutes of misery once a month, I would have to trudge through forty-five minutes of monthly professional development focused on the few teachers who felt sorry for me and supported me through the discussions. I knew in my heart that something had to change. I needed to somehow hook the staff in a new way, beyond a good professional book or video, so that they would be inspired by their own learning and make some changes in their teaching.

At this same point, the star-packed movie *Empire Falls* was being filmed in Waterville, just minutes from our school. Paul Newman, Ed Harris, and Helen Hunt were all in the production, to name just a few of the cast. My shallow side emerged, and I became intrigued (okay, obsessed) with the filming of the movie and catching glimpses of Paul Newman.

On the first day of filming, I missed Paul by minutes, but the excitement of the lights, cameras, and energy of the crowd made me want to stay and look on as the film crew bustled around. A man from the crowd turned around and asked me, "So what is this movie about?"

This was an interesting question, because Richard Russo's book is about life in a depressed community after the closures of once-prosperous paper mills. Russo teaches at Colby College, an upscale private college in Waterville. In fact, the community depicted in the book closely resembles our small city. I couldn't help but wonder how many people in the crowd had read the book. This film was not going to be a glamorous portrayal of the city they called home.

After several weeks as an unsuccessful stalker, I finally got to watch Paul Newman film a scene late one afternoon. He was high up on a ladder, perched on the side of a church, looking down as I stared up. I stood motionless, in silence, as I watched the sun beam down, casting a shadow on the man, the steeple, the step on which he was poised. He was standing awkwardly on the ladder, smoking a cigarette, looking off in the distance. I was fixed in the moment, this moment I had been chasing the last few weeks.

I was immediately brought back to reality by the jarring sounds of the neighborhood. A woman twenty feet away was yelling, raving about the cars being parked in front of her apartment building. Many heads turned her way. A young girl stood screaming at her mother, demanding to go to a friend's house. Her hysterics made even Paul Newman glance her way. The loud rumblings of a motorcycle filled the air and forced the director to shout, "Cut!" and halt filming for the moment.

Then there were the three fifth-grade girls from our school perched on the curb watching these stars in their backyard. They sat quietly with their hands resting on their chins as the film crew scurried around the church scene. Even the "tough" girls from school couldn't escape the magical spell of the filming of *Empire Falls*.

When else would you find Paul Newman and Ed Harris hanging out on Water Street, one of the shabbiest parts of town? I was struck with guilt. Even though I have taught at the school for many years, this was the first time I had ventured into the neighborhood, and it took Paul Newman to get me here. Why had I never been down here in the fifteen years I had worked in Waterville? I was ashamed at what lured me to really stop and look around at the neighborhood so many of our students called home. I began to wonder about the stories of the students who lived here. How much do we really know about the students we work with? How much do they know about us? This moment of watching Paul Newman high on that ladder on Water Street became my inspiration for the creation of "My Life in Seven Stories."

The Beginning of "My Life in Seven Stories"

At the first staff meeting in September teachers came into the library carrying their copies of the *Revision Toolbox* (Heard 2002), our new common staff text for the year. I had given the book out in June in case anyone wanted to read it over the summer. I also had journals laid out on all the tables. Teachers now knew the routine and took a journal. I could see the same passive body language that I had left them with last June. I was nervous. Instead of starting with my usual philosophical question about writing, I asked a personal question. "If you had only seven stories to tell of your life, what would they be? How would these stories reflect your life and define who you are as a person? Would one of your stories be the birth of your first child, or would it be a simple moment, like hiking alone through the woods? What are your seven stories?" Next, I asked everyone to open their journals and generate a list of possible titles that they could write about over the course of the year. Here is a sample list generated by a teacher:

- Childhood Play
- Listening/Observing
- Lost in Books
- Loving Myself
- Connecting
- Family
- Blessed

The attention and interest of the staff was captured immediately. I introduced staff to the concept of "snapshot writing." Barry Lane (1995) refers to this as short writing that captures the details of a moment in time. Even that first day, teachers were eager to share their stories. They smiled as they listened to one another reminisce about the significant moments in their lives.

During the first few weeks of September you could hear chatter among the staff in the hallways and in the lunchroom. Everywhere you turned,

SAMPLE TEACHER SNAPSHOTS

Snapshot of a Special Person, Written by a Grade 5 Teacher

Like a faucet that can't be turned off (frozen in love) she gives. She gives her time. She runs from event to event, giving her talents, energy, and heart. No one is too small. No one is too dumb. Rich and poor, liked and unliked, desired and undesired, it matters not. She gives. She pours out simple offerings of words and the quiet of listening. She dribbles useful things—a hairbrush, a pair of pants—into a life of need. She lavishes objects that let people know she wants you to do more than survive, she wants you to live.

Snapshot "Waiting," Written by a Grade 5 Teacher

They say patience is a virtue. If the waiting doesn't kill me, then I will be the epitome of the virtuous woman. You might say I was working for extra credit in virtuosity this past Friday.

My husband and I had a full weekend planned, and time was of the essence. We had sixty-four hours, and at least eighteen of them had to be behind the wheel of a car. High-gear me hit the ground running Friday afternoon.

I flew from school, leaving behind what I hoped would prepare me for Monday morning. By 3:30 I was home and ready. My husband said we could leave between 3:30 and 4:00. My head was pounding as I sucked down liquid caffeine and finished packing up the suitcase. 4:00 came and no Todd. I engaged the clock in a staring contest. The minutes crept by. I lost the battle with the clock. I grew grumpier and more selfish with every passing second. "Where is he? And he wants me to drive? This is so typical! I am glad we don't have to catch a plane." The language buzz of the questions filled my head.

The phone rang at 4:10, and the apology came along with promises of only thirty minutes to wait.

Finally at 5:00 we pulled out of the driveway. The car was very quiet, and I learned that I'm not as virtuous as I would like to be.

Figure 3.1

teachers were talking about their stories and how hard it would be to choose only seven. Even the art teacher was intrigued by the project. Early on she came to me and commented that she had written down the titles of her seven stories and that none of them involved her husband or son. "Is there something wrong with me?" she asked.

The monthly meetings were designed with predictable repetition. Teachers, administrators, and support staff were asked to generate short snapshots so that they could work with their own writing as a vehicle to explore revision strategies. Finding the resources for the staff—*The*

Figure 3.2

SAMPLE OF A STAFF MEETING AGENDA

Talking About Writing
November Staff Meeting
7:15–8:00 A.M.

- **Writer's Notebook (Individually)**

  "My Life in Seven Stories"

  If you could choose only seven stories that define/reflect who you are and your life, what would they be?
  - Brainstorm a list of possible snapshots
  - Write Snapshot #3
  - Revisit Snapshot #2—Write three alternative leads for the snapshot

- **Video: *Talking About Writing*, J. Portalupi and R. Fletcher (Whole Group)**
  - Conferencing: the heart of teaching writing (3 minutes)

- ***Talking About Writing* (Small Group)**
  - Share samples of student writing from your classroom
  - What are the strengths in the piece of student writing?
  - Share strategies for conferencing with students on writing

- ***The Revision Toolbox*, G. Heard (Resource)**
  - Peer conferencing revision questions

  Try out the conferencing questions with a student. Bring student writing and conference success stories to next staff meeting

- **Share (Whole Group)**

Revision Toolbox by Georgia Heard (2002) and the *Talking About Writing* videos by JoAnn Portalupi and Ralph Fletcher (2003)—was the easy part. The challenge would be to shift the exploration of writing strategies from the walls of the staff meeting to writing instruction.

In the Midst of Our Learning

At staff meetings, we worked on personal stories, viewed video segments, and examined samples of student writing from classrooms. We were working together to improve ourselves as writers and as writing teachers. We looked at student writing to inform our teaching.

Each session I introduced a revision strategy that I pulled from the gurus on writing. I used the work of Ralph Fletcher, Georgia Heard, Lucy

Figure 3.3

SOURCES FOR REVISION STRATEGIES

- **Titles**

  Craft Lessons, R. Fletcher and J. Portalupi

- **Word Choice**

  What a Writer Needs, R. Fletcher

  Craft Lessons, R. Fletcher and J. Portalupi

  Revision Toolbox, G. Heard

- **Adding Details**

  Revision Toolbox, G. Heard

- **Alternative Leads**

  The No-Nonsense Guide to Teaching Writing, J. Davis and S. Hill

  Craft Lessons, R. Fletcher and J. Portalupi

  Revision Toolbox, G. Heard

- **Alternative Endings**

  What a Writer Needs, R. Fletcher

  Craft Lessons, R. Fletcher and J. Portalupi

- **Cutting Words**

  Craft Lessons, R. Fletcher and J. Portalupi

- **Sentence Structure**

  Wondrous Words, K. Wood Ray

  Revision Toolbox, G. Heard

- **Change of Genre**

  Revision Toolbox, G. Heard

  The Multigenre Research Paper, C. Allen

Calkins, and Katie Wood Ray, to name a few. Each month staff tried out the revision strategy by revisiting one of the snapshots that they had written at an earlier meeting. I always provided a copy of one of my snapshots as a model that included the strategy we had explored as a group.

Over the course of the year we explored the revision strategies of titles, word choice, adding details, alternative leads, alternative endings, cutting words, sentence structure, and changing genres. I always asked staff to generate three alternatives for the strategy we were exploring.

I started the story shown in Figure 3.4 in my writer's notebook at a staff meeting. It was then used as a model to introduce the revision strat-

MODELING WRITING IN THE WORKSHOP

Magic Words: A True Story

Those magic words "Focus and pay attention" still haunt me. I often heard those magic words as a child. Those words now ring through my ears as I *reflect* back on last Thursday.

It started as an ordinary Thursday. I left my house with coffee in hand after hugs and kisses with my son Benjamin. I was quite focused on my day ahead but knew that I should stop for gasoline before heading off to Waterville.

So, I stopped to pump gas. I was pumping away, thinking about work. Since I had put the gas pump on automatic with the metal clip, I allowed my thoughts to drift miles away. Somewhere between thoughts, I decided that $10.00 would be enough gas and made the decision not to fill the tank. It was at this moment that I yanked the nozzle from my car.

Seconds passed before my thoughts returned to the task at hand. It was then that I realized that gas was still flowing, actually *gushing* out of the hose. *Why wouldn't the gas stop? What was wrong with this gas pump?* I stood there muttering to myself as gas continued to spray the side of my car.

The hose was out of control, spraying everywhere. Spraying my car, spraying me! I looked down only to watch the gas spray the bottom of my new skirt, and as I looked at my skirt, the nozzle squirted toward the sleeve of my jacket. In this same blurry moment I also felt the sensation of gas seeping into my black leather clogs. I couldn't figure out how to turn off the pump.

Then it all clicked. I remembered that I had used the clip to put the gas on automatic. I released the clip and the gas stopped flowing. I stood with the nozzle still in hand, standing in a pool of gasoline. I was mortified with embarrassment. I wondered how many people had witnessed this disaster.

How much time passed? I don't know. I do know that instead of $10.00, I now owed $12.49. I put the gasoline nozzle away and gracefully walked toward the store, *muttering* to myself those magic words that I heard so often as a child: "Focus and pay attention."

Revision Strategy: Word Choice

Think	Pouring	Cursing
1. Wonder	1. Spraying	1. Talking
2. Ponder	2. Gushing*	2. Screaming
3. Reflect*	3. Flowing	3. Muttering*
*Words selected for final draft		

Figure 3.4

egy of word choice to staff. Participants were asked to select a snapshot they had written and to choose three words they could revise, brainstorming alternatives for each word selected.

Small Moments of Encouragement

Staff meetings had taken on a predictable structure that promoted learning and fluency through the use of personal writing. One month I introduced the revision strategy of alternative leads. I asked staff to revisit a snapshot and highlight their lead sentence to write three alternative ways they could start their story. At the end, as usual, I asked if anyone would like to share.

Donald, a fourth-grade teacher, raised his hand. I was surprised because he hadn't shared yet this year. I would consider him a "resistant" learner. But, as Donald began to speak, his story was told through his first lead sentence, "My junior high school experience was like the part of a VCR tape that you would rather have erased." The writing continued in the same emotionally wrenching style. Not a sound could be heard in the room before he broke in with, "Do you get a mood from that? Well, that's all I am going to read." I knew at that moment that we were breaking ground and that the culture of the staff was beginning to change, even if teachers were not recognizing this new learning and experimentation with writing. We were beginning to tell our stories as colleagues and writers.

Instructional Strategies Moving into Classrooms

One day in January, I encountered three different teachers talking about how they had tried out the revision strategy that I had just modeled at the staff meeting earlier that morning with their students. It was the first time that I was seeing new learning from staff meetings seep into classroom instruction. I began to see firsthand the power of teachers as writers. I realized that having teachers write was an essential component in our professional development.

Cathy, a fifth-grade teacher, caught me at the end of one day. She was excited to show me the work she had been doing in her classroom. Cathy had shared one of her original snapshots about sledding with her daughter with her students. She explained how she used this piece of personal writing to launch a study in personal narrative with them. I was thrilled to see a teacher modeling her own writing with students.

While some teachers were dabbling with new revision strategies on their own, others were asking me to model the same strategies that I had introduced at staff meetings to their students. As a result of this request I began introducing "My Life in Seven Stories" to students as a unit of study in revision. It was a trial run to see if this same model worked with kids.

CATHY'S FINAL DRAFT OF SNAPSHOT

I am sitting on a red plastic sled in my pajamas. I did have enough sense to put on my twenty-year-old Sorels (without socks, of course), a part of my past that I refuse to leave behind. As I sit here on this cold, tiny sled, two thoughts come to mind. The first is that my rear end is wedged in so tightly, I fear that when I get up, the sled will be stuck permanently to my backside, and the second is that this is the moment that reminds me of a day twenty years ago, living in the Aspen mountains. The same boots warmed my toes. The same sun radiates such warmth that I feel closer to it than I should on a December day in central Maine. It feels more like April. A brilliant blue sky above contrasts with the stark whiteness where I sit watching Olivia play in the snow for the first time. She looks like an Eskimo, only her fat, red cheeks glowing, as she squints her eyes in the brilliant light. She just wants to sit here. So we sit; my ever-so-patient, understanding husband, and my strong-willed, determined daughter.

    She smiles as her daddy throws snow, makes a baby snowman, and tries everything he knows to get her to move. She is content to sit and look at the snow, taking off her mittens to feel the icy cold melt between her fingers. I am content to sit and watch the scene before me. The only sound is the snap of the shutter each time I take a picture, catching a glimpse of her pure, joyful spirit.

    This moment defines me. I am where I always dreamed I would be. I wouldn't want to be anywhere else on this earth right now. I'm in my backyard enjoying the beauty of my world with my family. *I am happy to be sitting on a red plastic sled in my pajamas.*

Figure 3.5

I wasn't sure if fifth graders could really define who they were or share stories of significance. How wrong I was! It wasn't long before I realized that fourth and fifth graders could write more freely and without inhibitions than adults. On the second day Katy wrote,

> *I can't sleep, the yelling is shaking the house. My sister Jasmine is in the hallway listening. I bet that is the only time she really listens.*
>
> *My dad drinks a lot, and when he does he lies about it. He would drink up to ten days in a row. My dad has left a few times but he always comes back. My mom hates it when he drinks. Sometimes I feel that he is not there, that something else is.*
>
> *I hear the words, the words I hate the most. "Good-bye." My dad walked out and slammed the door. I ran down the stairs bawling. My mom is sitting at the table. I walk over and give her a hug.*

Not all the writing was gut wrenching. Many students wrote with voice and energy about events that would be insignificant to me as an adult, but were important, humorous, or inspiring to a ten-year-old:

Dad's Right Tire
Grade 4 Student
It was morning and my dad gave Mandy and me a morning wakeup call with pots and pans. Bang! Bang! Bang! "Wake up sleepy heads, time for school," he called. Mandy and I pushed him out of the living room again, as I was thinking that I would have my revenge. Then my mom came in the room and said, "Leave them alone." So he did.

Then he went to work. On the way to work, he was about two miles away from Dead River when he noticed a tire roll out in front of his truck. He kept driving. Then he had a funny feeling about something. So, he stopped the truck and checked all his tires. To his horror he saw that his right passenger tire was gone! Now he knows that the tire that rolled by was really his!

Later when he told Mandy and me the story, we cracked up laughing. We figured his bad luck was his payback for waking us up so early with the banging of pots and pans. Oh yeah, just in case you are wondering—he never did get the tire back!

Fuzzy
Grade 4 Student
On a dark and rainy day, my friend Mitch got a new haircut. I just had an urge to touch it! I waited until the end of the day to do it. Not telling anyone about it. I just had to. So when he turned around to get his stuff I did it! It was right before vacation. Then I'd never get a chance to touch it. It was now or never. So he turned around and that's when I did it. I just had to do it. So I did, and it was FUZZY!

The Uh-Oh Word!
Grade 4 Student
One afternoon I was going back to my aunt's house. I was trying to buckle up my little cousin. I said, "Crap, this is hard to do!" Then my cousin said the word crap. *I said, "No, don't say that word."*

So we left from the mall and headed home. Then once I got home there was a message on the answering machine. It was my aunt saying, "Trisha, thanks for teaching Noah the C-R-A-P word. He dropped a spoon on the floor and for five minutes straight he's been saying, 'crap, crap, crap, crap, crap'!"

The Adventure of the Burnt Pie
Grade 4 Student
Have you ever made anything without your parents? Well I have! It all started in the kitchen making an apple pie. I had flour and stuff all over me. I went into the living room to watch television. I was in the middle of my favorite show when I smelled something funny. The smell of fire was in the air. I forgot the T.V. and darted into the kitchen like a cheetah chasing its prey.

All of a sudden fire alarms were going off. All I could hear was beep, beep, beep. There were flames two feet high coming out of the stove. I was biting my fingernails. "Mom," I screamed with horror. My mom ran into the kitchen with the fire extinguisher high above her head. I thought she was running toward me so I took three giant steps away from the stove. She was yelling so much I couldn't even hear a word she was saying. She had a huge blue vein popping out of her forehead and her face was beet red.

"Katelyn, get out of the kitchen," she screamed. I just stood there like I didn't hear. "Get out," she screamed again. She yelled so loud I bet the neighbors could hear next door. I ran out of the kitchen in a hurry. I peeked into the kitchen just a little bit. I saw my mom spraying the apple pie with the gooey white stuff.

When the fire was out I went back into the kitchen. The pie was freezing cold and squishy. "That takes care of that," said my mom.

"So I am off the hook?" I asked.

"No," she said. "You are grounded!"

That's how my solo baking adventure ended.

I knew at this moment that the work that we were doing in the area of writing was powerful, and that instructional practices in classrooms were changing. The same teachers who had been resisting the format of the staff meetings were beginning to dabble in "My Life in Seven Stories" with their students. The modeling that I was doing in a few rooms was once again filtering into new classrooms. Teachers were sharing the nuts and bolts of implementing this idea with one another. Some bought journals for the project; other teachers simply provided one-subject notebooks for students to use as writer's notebooks.

The students certainly had stories of significance to tell. Stories ranged from getting glasses, scary phone calls, and meeting best friends, to parents getting divorced. Their stories were real, and they were compelled to write them down. Students, like teachers, felt limited with writing only seven stories from their lives.

Here is a sample of a title list generated by a grade 5 Title I student:

- First Goal in Soccer
- Meeting Ashley
- Mom and Dad Splitting Up
- My Friend Brittany Moving Away
- Florida
- Bye-Bye Fish
- The Scary Call!

I created a predictable structure for students when I worked with them, mirroring my work in staff meetings. I wanted students to be clear on expectations and feel comfortable with the routine so that they too could become more fluent in using the strategies they learned. The goal was for students to learn revision strategies so they would be able to use them independently during writing workshop. Students were asked to generate a list of possible stories that they could later select from for their "Life in Seven Stories." They then spent time orally sharing their stories with their classmates before moving on. Sharing orally helped students articulate the significance of their stories.

The Nuts and Bolts of Classroom Implementation: A Three-Day Writing Cycle

Day One: Writing Our Stories

I used a three-day cycle for launching "My Life in Seven Stories" in any classroom. On day one, I shared a draft of one of my stories as a model. I wanted students to hear my struggles as a writer and to hear my stories as a person. Students then chose a story from their title list and wrote a snapshot. If students finished early, they were encouraged to go back and add to or delete from their original brainstormed list of stories or share their writing with a peer. The first day of the cycle was always my favorite, because students were immersed in writing that was significant to them.

MY SNAPSHOT MODEL TO USE IN CLASSROOMS

Spider-man

In this picture it is the middle of summer with a temperature of 90 degrees outside. Benjamin is Spider-man. Halloween is nowhere in sight. He has just taken a break from running through my garden in search of spiders. At times this summer I even forgot that he was often in full costume.

I am reminded of the night at Sarah's café when I suddenly noticed that people were looking toward our table. I looked at Ben and Samantha to make sure that they were acting appropriately. Ben was sitting quietly, slurping up his spaghetti. Sam was sound asleep in her carrier. I looked at Ben again. This time I was the one who was smiling. It was then that I realized that my son was dressed in his full Spider-man attire, entertaining those seated at the tables around us.

Figure 3.6

STUDENT-GENERATED SNAPSHOTS FROM DAY ONE OF CYCLE

Bye-Bye Fish

It was my birthday. One of Steven's friends gave me a fish tank and my mom bought me fish. I had two angel fish, one shark fish, and an algae eater. One of my angel fish was named Boo. Boo went behind the green plant in the tank and twenty minutes later Boo died. But I still had Dow the other angel fish, Fang the shark fish, and Food the algae eater.

When I came home from school the next day there was a big hole in my tank. All of the water was on the carpet. My fish were all dead. I ran in my room, gagged for air, and cried really hard. Then I wiped my eyes and went back down the stairs and helped Jamie pick up the dead fish and flush them down the toilet. Then I threw out the tank and the gravel. Our house smelled like rotten eggs. It was sad but smelly. I really missed Boo, Dow, Fang, and Food. Bye-bye Fish!

Lady in the Window

"I'm going to catch you and then you will be it. I'm on your tail."

All of a sudden my friend Adrian was on my next door neighbor's lawn. She was right in the window. I thought to myself, is he nuts?

She knocks on the window. All I could see was her wrinkly old skin with curlers in her hair. We ran in horror with sweat dripping down our face. She was one scary woman!

Figure 3.7

Day Two: Revision Strategy Introduced

On day two I introduced a revision strategy. I would always bring out the snapshot I had shared the day before. We also reviewed mentor texts that demonstrated the craft of writing that we were exploring. For my snapshot titled "Spider-man" I introduced the strategy of word choice.

I shared sample sentences from a few mentor texts that I had copied for the overhead that demonstrated how the author's word choices brought the sentences off the pages of the book and into the reader's mind. I wanted the students to know that simple words can be powerful and that more sophisticated vocabulary doesn't always make for better writing:

- "Now a school of goldfish could go swimming in the pool of drool that dog makes while he is sleeping." Katherine Hannigan, *Ida B* (2004, p. 4)
- "Those hotdogs were a mean lump in the middle of my stomach, sloshing around with a Mountain Dew." Patricia Reilly Giff, *Pictures of Hollis Woods* (2002, p. 5)
- "One morning at school in late February, he dared this little kid, Paul Anniboli, to lick the ice-cold metal bar on the jungle gym. Of course the kid's tongue got stuck there, frozen solid to the metal. 'Don't move!' Teddy told him, but of course the kid panicked and pulled away and left a bunch of tongue skin stuck to the metal pole." Ralph Fletcher, *Fig Pudding* (1995, p. 50)
- "I found Mom and Dad at the small kitchen table, leaning against each other, eyes closed, tears running down their faces. Dad's shoulders were shaking. He grabbed his gut, as if in pain. Mom was red-faced, gasping for breath. Some new ingredient! Mom choked, and they both let out a howl of laughter, almost a scream, a wild animal sound startled me as it rang out and bounced off the walls and brought the other kids in our family into the kitchen." Ralph Fletcher, *Fig Pudding* (1995, p. 135)

I reread my writing for students and underlined three words in the snapshot that I thought I could improve to help the reader create a more vivid picture of the event. I then invited students to help me think of at least three alternative words for each word circled. In the end I chose the word choices that I would use in my final draft. Students were then asked to circle three words in their writing that they might want to revisit and to generate alternative word choices. It was expected that they would always create three new alternative ideas for the strategy we were exploring.

MY MODEL INTRODUCING WORD CHOICE STRATEGY

Spider-man

In this picture it is the middle of summer with a temperature of 90 degrees outside. Benjamin is Spider-man. Halloween is nowhere in sight. He has just taken a break from <u>running</u> through my garden in search of spiders. At times this summer I even forgot that he was often in full costume.

I am reminded of the night at Sarah's café when I suddenly noticed that people were <u>looking</u> toward our table. I looked at Ben and Samantha to make sure that they were acting appropriately. Ben was sitting quietly, slurping up his spaghetti. Sam was sound asleep in her carrier. I looked at Ben again. This time I was the one who was <u>smiling</u>. It was then that I realized that my son was dressed in his full Spider-man attire, entertaining those seated at the tables around us.

Alternative Word Choices Generated with Students

Running	Looking	Smiling
1. Sprinting	1. Glancing	1. Giggling
2. Bounding	2. Staring	2. Chuckling
3. Swerving	3. Nodding	3. Smirking

Figure 3.8

Day Three: Peer Conference

On day three I brought out my snapshot once again. This time I shared the revision ideas I had created. We then had a large-group peer conference on my writing. I asked the class to identify a strength in my writing as well as an area I might want to go back and revisit. Students broke into pairs and had a general peer conference on the strengths and needs of their own writing. The student authors were asked to write the strength and weakness that their partner shared with them on a Post-it. Having the student authors write the Post-it themselves helped them to be more active listeners during the conference. It also helped the peer listener articulate the elements of what they thought made good writing. Students then went back to their seats and made any changes they wanted to.

Students were assessed on the revision strategy that had been introduced and for having had the peer conference and the Post-it on their writing. Students would then rewrite or type up their snapshot as a final draft for their "Life in Seven Stories" book (see Figure 3.11 for a sample assessment rubric). The three-day writing cycle repeated itself through the eight strategies, applying a new revision strategy to each snapshot. As students

STUDENT SNAPSHOTS, DAY TWO, WORD CHOICE

Bye-Bye Fish

It was my birthday. One of Steven's friends gave me a fish tank and my mom bought me fish. I had two angel fish, one shark fish, and an algae eater. One of my angel fish was named Boo. Boo went behind the green plant in the tank and twenty minutes later Boo <u>died.</u> But I still had Dow the other angel fish, Fang the shark fish, and Food the algae eater.

When I came home from school the next day there was a big hole in my tank. All of the water was on the carpet. My fish were all dead. I ran in my room, <u>gagged</u> for air, and cried really hard. Then I wiped my eyes and went back down the stairs and helped Jamie pick up the <u>dead</u> fish and flush them down the toilet. Then I threw out the tank and the gravel. Our house smelled like rotten eggs. It was sad but smelly. I really missed Boo, Dow, Fang, and Food. Bye-bye Fish!

Alternative Word Choices Generated by the Student

Died	Gagged	Dead
1. Bit the dust	1. Choked	1. Lifeless*
2. Kicked the bucket*	2. Coughed	2. Smelly
3. Floated	3. Begged for air*	3. Stiff

*Word chosen for the final draft

Lady in the Window (Revision Strategy of Adding Details by "Cracking Open a Line")

"I'm going to catch you and then you will be it. I'm on your tail."

All of a sudden my friend Adrian was on my next door neighbor's lawn. She was right in the window. I thought to myself, is he nuts?

<u>She knocks on the window.</u> All I could see was her wrinkly old skin with curlers in her hair. We ran in horror with sweat dripping down our face. She was one scary woman!

Alternative Lines Generated by the Student

1. She knocks on the window like a stampede.
2. She knocks on the window like drums beating crazy.*
3. She knocks on the window like bees stinging her.

*Alternate line chosen for final draft.

Figure 3.9

progressed through the project, we found that they were beginning to make revisions independently, even beyond the revision strategies that they were exploring.

PEER REVISION CONFERENCE PROCEDURE

- **Student Author Reads Snapshot to a Classmate**

- **Classmate Identifies:**
  + Strength
  - Area that is unclear or confusing

- **Author Writes Conference Notes on a Post-it**
  + Strength
  - Area that is unclear or confusing

REVISION STRATEGY: WORD CHOICE

Expectation	Does Not Meet	Partially Meets	Meets	Exceeds
Three Words Underlined to Be Revised				
Three Alternative Word Choices for Each Underlined Word				
New Word Choices Used in Final Draft				
Post-its from the Revision Conference				

SNAPSHOTS OF PEER CONFERENCES

Teacher Snapshot: Spider-man Conference Modeled in Front of the Class
+ Students said that they could visualize Ben being dressed up as Spider-man catching spiders. They especially liked the word change of *sprinting* from *running*.
- Students thought I could rework my lead sentence and take away the words "In this picture …"

Student Snapshot: Bye-Bye Fish Peer Conference
+ Peers said they really liked the new wording of *lifeless*. They thought the snapshot had good description.
- Peer wanted to know more about the hole in the tank. How did the hole get there?

Student Snapshot: Lady in the Window
+ Peers said they liked when he said they ran away.
- Peer wanted more details at the end.

In the End

Students and staff began sharing their stories with each other in the hallways and in lines for the bus. I believe the power of the project was the parallel learning of teachers and students, moving beyond the walls of the staff meetings into classrooms. Teachers began to take new risks in the area of writing instruction. They were able to immediately apply new strategies and use the support network of their peers as they encountered obstacles.

Most striking to many of us were the gains students made in the two classrooms where "My Life in Seven Stories" was used throughout the year. These were our fourth- and fifth-grade intervention classrooms—students who had fallen at least a year or more behind their peers in literacy achievement by the time they reached the upper elementary grades (see Chapter 5). Throughout the year, I worked in these classrooms with teachers and students each month, modeling the strategies through the three-day cycle. Many of these students made greater gains in a year than they had in the previous three years combined (see Figure 3.13).

Figure 3.13

DATA FROM LOCAL WRITING ASSESSMENT USING A PROMPT

Grade 4 Intervention Classroom	Grade 5 Intervention Classroom
September (Before "My Life in Seven Stories")	**September (Before "My Life in Seven Stories")**
100% of the students did not meet the standard in writing.	100% of the students did not meet the standard in writing.
0% of the students partially met the standard in writing.	0% of the students partially met the standard in writing.
0% of the students met the standard in writing.	0% of the students met the standard in writing.
0% of the students exceeded the standard in writing.	0% of the students exceeded the standard in writing.
June (After "My Life in Seven Stories")	**June (After "My Life in Seven Stories")**
50% of the students did not meet the standard in writing.	16% of the students did not meet the standard in writing.
43% of the students partially met the standard in writing.	68% of the students partially met the standard in writing.
7% of the students met the standard in writing.	16% of the students met the standard in writing.
0% of the students exceeded the standard in writing.	0% of the students exceeded the standard in writing.

I have spent time reflecting on why this model of professional development was successful. The project evolved over time and engaged teachers with a topic that hooked them—stories of their lives. I would be lying if I told you that I designed the project within a solid theoretical framework. Only upon reflection can I go back and identify the theoretical framework and research base that supports the success of this program:

- Gradual Release Model (Pearson and Gallagher 1983)
  This model was created by Pearson and Gallagher and later adapted by Sweeney (2002) for staff development. In this model the staff developer provides direct instruction. Gradually, through guided practice, the responsibility and application of new learning shifts from the staff developer to the teacher. In "My Life in Seven Stories," I modeled the revision strategies for teachers but gradually released the responsibility to them as learners and writers.
- Reflective Inquiry (Pinnell and Rodgers 2004)
  Reflective inquiry is a critical component to effective staff development. The model promotes learning through inquiry and self-discovery. Although I provided models and resources, teachers were active learners within the process, constantly evaluating their teaching and learning through analyzing their own writing development.
- Predictable Structure (Graves 1994)
  Donald Graves advocates for a predictable structure within the learning community, and he is one of a long line of researchers who support workshop environments with clear routines and expectations that don't vary over time. Our teachers too needed a predictable structure. Staff meetings took on a predictable format, with everyone knowing what to expect each month.
- Common Staff Resources (Sweeney 2003)
  Dianne Sweeney writes about the importance of common staff resources to create a common understanding of new learning. We had a number of core texts available to everyone, including *The Revision Toolbox*, excerpts from *Craft Lessons*, and *The Writing Workshop*. *Talking About Writing* videos were used to spark discussions. These resources provided us with common language so that we could begin to create a common base of understanding of best practice in writing.
- Repetition to Gain Fluency of Strategies (Allington 2000)
  Richard Allington writes about the importance of repetition so that students can gain fluency and independence. I believe this is also true for adult learners. To change instructional practices in the classroom,

teachers too need many opportunities to play with new ideas over time so that they become fluent with them.

- Short Writing (Lane 1995)
  Barry Lane refers to "snapshot writing" as short writing that captures moments of time and zooms in on sharp details. This form of "snapshot" writing became a tool for teachers to write about their own lives. Short writing enabled us to be able to rework our writing instruction within the time constraints of a monthly forty-five-minute staff meeting.

Has the staff turned around to the point of welcoming professional development during staff meetings? Absolutely not!

My moment of basking in self-glory lasted literally a moment. I was given a quick shot of reality when one of the teachers glanced up from her assessment sheet at the last staff meeting of the year and asked, "So, when is this all going away? When is Harriet going to change staff meetings back to the way they were?" Before I knew it, three teachers were reminiscing happily about the way it used to be. I was zapped, deflated, and speechless.

Despite the enthusiasm for and enjoyment of the new strategies learned, the connections between colleagues, and the thrill of writing something personally valuable, many still want to go back to "the way it used to be." However, the professional conversations, changes in instructional practices, and student learning are clear evidence that we can't go back to the way it used to be. The learning and changes are real even if not all the teachers value the learning in the same way I do. A year later teachers and students are still speaking the same language when it comes to writing instruction, exploring revision strategies, and, best yet, sharing new stories of success and struggles.

What started out as an innovative in-house staff development strategy became an ongoing professional conversation. Our writing helped us learn a little more about one another. By telling our stories, we created a climate where students and staff were safe to learn, take risks, and share their stories, the very stories that molded us into the writers we are today.

CHAPTER FOUR

Study Groups: Developing Voluntary Professional Development Programs

Remember that in the end it will be teachers who make a difference in children's school lives. It is teachers who will either lead the change or resist and stymie it. The focus of school change has to be on supporting teachers in their efforts to become more expert and reorganizing all the aspects of the educational system so that they can teach as expertly as they know how.

RICHARD ALLINGTON

As a teacher, I often found that my needs and interests were not met within the allotted in-service days designated for professional development during the school year. I was thirsty for professional development opportunities involving new instructional practices. Instead, I found that most of our in-service days were planned months in advance to address state assessment requirements.

I had a conversation about this with the assistant superintendent. He too believed that teachers needed opportunities to direct their own learning. He explained the four-tier system for professional development: "Jen, there are many professional demands that need to be met. We need to meet federal mandates, state requirements, district goals, and then there are the individual professional goals of teachers. It's all a matter of juggling responsibilities, balancing time, and prioritizing needs." His explanation made sense, but I was still frustrated because my individual professional needs were at the bottom of the priority list. Year after year I found that our in-service days were preplanned at the district level, leaving no time for teachers to choose topics of their own interest to explore with colleagues.

Meeting the Individual Professional Needs of Teachers

One of my first initiatives as literacy specialist was to offer teachers an opportunity to come together and share their thinking around reading and writing. I started small. I sent an e-mail asking if anyone would like to meet as a group to explore the concept of student literature discussions. I told the teachers I would purchase the resources—all they needed to do was show up. (I confess that I did go around to a few teachers and personally invite them to be part of the group, in case no one volunteered.)

In my first solicitation five years ago, eight teachers volunteered to meet monthly to talk about literature circles, using the text *Literature Circles* by Harvey Daniels. Back then we didn't have a name for what we were doing. We just got together once a month and learned about literature circles, sharing our experiences as we tried implementing them with our students.

At the end of the year teachers asked what I was going to offer next. Even with all of the demands being placed on their time, they wanted to participate in future study groups held after school. Teachers found that this was time well spent. They enjoyed the informal time spent conversing with their colleagues. Teachers completed a written evaluation, where I asked them to rate this form of professional development. One teacher responded, "On a scale of 1 to 5 this is definitely a 5! When we read and reflect using the tools that the children will use, we become more proficient in the tool. It saves the children from the 'learn as you go' approach that we have to use when we want to try something new with our class. Much of the troubleshooting and professional discussion can happen as we flow in and out of the roles of learner, participant, and teacher."

At the end of the first year, I asked teachers what literacy topics they would like to see offered the following year. Teachers provided ideas, and study groups were organized in response to their desires. Now I offer an average of five different study groups a year with about twenty-five teachers (out of twenty-eight in the school) participating in at least one study group.

First impressions are lasting. I attribute the success of our study groups to starting small and following the lead of the teachers. Study groups are the hot buzz in professional development. Everywhere I look I can buy "packages" of predesigned study group materials. It's great to use available resources to guide professional development, but I am cautious about the packages that are being marketed, because it is critical that professional development opportunities be personalized to meet the needs of the staff. Otherwise, offerings will be no more personalized than the professional development opportunities that I experienced as a teacher.

What Should You Expect from a Study Group?

Study groups provide teachers with the opportunity to reflect, review, and integrate new thinking into their classroom instruction. Our study groups are not just about new activities to try tomorrow in the classroom. It's important that new literacy practices be integrated and fit within a cohesive literacy framework. During the study group sessions over the last few years, we've shifted the focus from trying new ideas to having teachers examine their own thinking. We use professional resources as springboards for discussions and personal examination.

As one teacher wrote, "My participation in the study group provided me the time to collaborate with my peers. The resources shared at the sessions gave me new insights into my teaching. Sharing ideas and working together also helped me to maintain focus and enthusiasm for what I was learning. This form of professional development gave me so much as a learner. I was actively involved in my own learning from start to finish. The support given by the group makes it safe and easy to try new things."

Recently a teacher came to me and shared that participation in a study group was part of her evaluation plan for the year. The school administrator asked the teacher for evidence of classroom changes that would document the participation in the study group. The administrator was looking for a measurable outcome. We hadn't started the study group, and the teacher wasn't sure what activities should be written as part of the plan. In the end she decided to document her thinking throughout the study group as evidence for the evaluation plan instead of listing activities from the study group book.

We are in an age of assessment frenzy. Everything needs to be measured, including teacher learning. Alfie Kohn notes in his book *What It Means to Be Well Educated* that we will never see the word *explore* as a standard because it can't be measured. Ellin Keene, in a recent talk at the National Council of Teachers of English annual meeting, reminded the audience about the importance of giving kids "think time." The same is true for teachers. One teacher told me the other day, "There is no time to think and process all these new reading and writing strategies and activities. I don't even know anymore what I should hold sacred as the core components of my literacy program. I just need time to think." Study groups provide this think time.

My Role in Study Groups

I am the hostess and party planner, working behind the scenes to organize the study groups. I solicit volunteers, find resources, set meeting dates, purchase refreshments, and copy materials and articles. Finally, I participate as an equal member of each group. I think the reason study groups work is that the teachers are directing their own learning. When asked what is important in a study group leader, a teacher participant responded, "First and foremost it is important that the person leading the group not teach. The group needs to be open so that everyone feels comfortable to talk and that no one person is the expert . . . we are all experts. I think when someone is talking at you then participants will not be as willing to share." Study groups will die a slow death if literacy specialists run them as traditional in-services, where attendance is mandatory and the organizer is looked at as the "expert." It is unspoken protocol that these are not gripe sessions, and the conversations need to stay positive and professional. That's not to say that we don't get a good joke in, or laugh often at one of our own classroom mishaps.

Finding a Focus and Resources

Every spring I start to organize the study groups for the following school year. I usually send out an e-mail asking teachers which literacy topics they are interested in exploring during the upcoming year and whether they wish to continue with the same study group topic. I always offer study groups on reading, writing, and word study. I have learned not to jump from topic to topic year by year. I usually stay with a topic for a few years so that we can gain a deeper understanding of the concepts explored. One of the groups that I am working with is on their third year of exploring strategic reading strategies using *Still Learning to Read* as their base text.

I find that the first year of a study group is more of an awareness and experimentation stage than long-term implementation. Teachers like the comfort associated with returning to a group and often wish to continue with the group for another year.

Every year I provide new resources even if we decide to focus on the same topic. I find new materials by looking through spring catalogs for new publications. I also use publisher Web sites to find ideas. A great professional development site that I use from Stenhouse Publishers is called *Read, Share, Teach* (RST) at www.stenhouse.com. This Web site provides free workshop ideas and facilitator notes.

It is important to have a focus for any study group, with supporting resources. Teachers have asked in the past to have a "sharing" group. A sharing group simply consists of teachers who meet monthly to share ideas and activities they are using in the classroom. I have tried sharing groups several times and each time sense that they never really get going or sustain momentum. The biggest issue is that the same few teachers bring something to share and the others just come to listen. Or, I bring materials to share as a backup and end up being the only one sharing, which defeats the structure of the study group. Again, the sharing groups become activity-sharing sessions, and as a whole they don't fit within a comprehensive literacy framework.

Figure 4.1
Sample e-mail outlining study group options.

Figure 4.1 shows a sample e-mail I send to teachers with the offerings for study groups.

STUDY GROUP OFFERINGS

I am beginning to organize study groups for next year. Let me know if you are interested in participating in any of the groups below. This will help me start ordering and collecting needed resources. Thanks, Jen

Creating Strategic Readers

Grades 3–5 (Afternoon Meetings)

This group will continue to work with the book *Still Learning to Read* by Franki Sibberson and Karen Szymusiak. It is designed for grades 3 and up. It focuses on comprehension strategies and getting students to be strategic readers. We will also be getting the authors' new videos that will complement the book and should be ready for the fall. You are welcome to jump into this group even if you did not participate this year.

Portfolio Group

Grades 3–5 (3 Whole-Day Releases)

This is an opportunity to reflect on how portfolios are being used in your classroom. The group this past year moved to a "progress-olio" that was used during parent/teacher conferences to document student learning. This group is a relaxed opportunity to redesign how you are using portfolios. There is no "right" way or predetermined outcome. Various portfolio designs will be shared. The group will kick off with a full-day release to read, share, and plan. The expectation is that you design a model that works for you. Professional journal articles and teacher-generated resources will be shared). (Meetings: full day in October, full day in November, full day in March)

Word Study

Grades 3–5 (Hall School—Morning Meetings)

This group will explore the topic of word study using the book by Max Brand called *Word Savvy*. He incorporates the work of Kathy Ganske's *Word Journeys* (assessment and word sorts) and provides a model of looking at word study throughout the teaching day. (Meetings: Monthly October–April)

Revision Strategies

Grade 3 (Mitchell School—Lunch Meeting)

This will be a lunch book group offered to third-grade teachers. We will meet monthly (October–April) to discuss and share teaching ideas around the book *The Revision Toolbox* by Georgia Heard.

Author Study on Andrew Clements

Grade 4 (Hall School)

The purpose of this group is to develop an author study on Andrew Clements. We will read a book a month and meet to share ideas on how we might use the books in our classrooms. The hope is that we can take away a binder of ideas, because we have selected Clements as our fourth-grade author study.

Writing Nonfiction

Grades 3–5 (Hall School)

This group will explore the topic of reading and writing nonfiction with students. We will look at the book *Is That a Fact?* by Tony Stead. We will also use his video series, *Time for Nonfiction*. The emphasis will be on teaching students to write nonfiction.

Figure 4.1
continued

Planning and Scheduling Groups

Study groups are organized each spring for the following year by the time we leave for summer break. I try to keep the groups small. I have found that six to eight participants per group works well. If too many teachers sign up for a group, I split them into two different study groups. Recently sixteen teachers signed up for a study group on strategic reading. I split the teachers into two groups. One study group comprised grade 3 and 4 teachers, and the other group consisted of grade 5 and special education teachers. I do not want to be seen as handpicking participants for the study groups, so I tend to split study groups by grade levels, not people.

Next I select study group meeting dates. Study groups don't start until October; we are all too busy starting the school year and administering fall assessments in September. Because study groups are voluntary, it is important that they work for the teachers' schedules.

If special education meetings are held on a certain day of the week, I try to stay away from that day. If our union meetings take place on the first Wednesday afternoon of the month, I stay away from that day. I am looking to maximize participation, and don't want to have teachers choosing between meetings. If the meeting is the first Thursday of the month, I try to stick to the first week of the month for the rest of the year. I avoid study group meetings in December. It tends to be a busy time of year. I end study groups in April, because May and June become crazy with administering spring assessments to students.

Study groups are scheduled in the mornings before school, during lunch, and after school. I schedule meetings at times that meet the teachers' preferences. One building that I work at has a veteran staff, most of whose children are grown and out of the house. These teachers come to school early. They welcome morning study groups before school, from 7:00 to 8:00 A.M. The other building I work at has a lot of teachers with young children. They don't come too early but will stay later after school, from 3:00 to 4:00 P.M. I have also offered study groups as a lunch meeting. They are shorter because of the constraints of lunch schedules (forty-five minutes). Knowing the staff helps me determine when to offer study groups.

Once study groups are organized, I let teachers know the schedule for the upcoming year. Teachers know the dates months in advance so that they can plan accordingly when scheduling doctor and dentist appointments. I provide teachers with a copy of the schedule before they leave for the summer, and give them an additional copy when they return to work

Figure 4.2

POSSIBLE BOOKS OR TOPICS FOR STUDY GROUPS

Spelling and Word Study

- *Word Savvy,* Max Brand
- *Spelling K–8,* Diane Snowball and Faye Bolton
- *Focus on Spelling* (video), Diane Snowball
- *Spelling Inquiry,* Kelly Chandler and the Mapleton Teacher-Research Group

Writing

- *Craft Lessons,* Ralph Fletcher and JoAnn Portalupi
- *Nonfiction Craft Lessons,* JoAnn Portalupi and Ralph Fletcher
- *When Students Write* (video), Ralph Fletcher and JoAnn Portalupi
- *The Writing Workshop,* Katie Wood Ray
- *Wondrous Words,* Katie Wood Ray
- *Is That a Fact?,* Tony Stead
- *The Revision Toolbox,* Georgia Heard

Literature Discussions

- *Literature Circles,* Harvey Daniels
- *Looking into Literature Circles* (video), Harvey Daniels

Reading Comprehension

- *Strategies That Work,* Stephanie Harvey and Anne Goudvis
- *Reading with Meaning,* Debbie Miller
- *Happy Reading!* (video), Debbie Miller
- *I Read It, but I Don't Get It,* Cris Tovani
- *Thoughtful Reading* (video), Cris Tovani
- *Still Learning to Read,* Franki Sibberson and Karen Szymusiak
- *Bringing Reading to Life* (video), Franki Sibberson and Karen Szymusiak

Struggling Readers

- *Supporting Struggling Readers and Writers,* Dorothy Strickland, Kathy Ganske, and Joanne Monroe
- *What Really Matters for Struggling Readers,* Richard Allington

Organizing for Literacy Instruction

- *The Art of Teaching Reading,* Lucy Calkins
- Journal articles from NCTE and IRA

Figure 4.3

SAMPLE OF STUDY GROUP SCHEDULE
GIVEN TO PARTICIPANTS

Creating Strategic Readers

Grades 3–5 (Hall School—Afternoon Meetings)
This group will continue to work with the book *Still Learning to Read* by Franki
Sibberson and Karen Szymusiak. It is geared toward grades 3 and up.

Participants: (List Names of Participants)
Time: 3:00–4:00
School: Albert S. Hall School
Place: Literacy Room
Dates:
    Thursday, October 14
    Thursday, November 10
    Thursday, January 13
    Thursday, February 10
    Thursday, March 10
    Thursday, April 7

in September. Principals are given copies of the study group dates to incorporate into the school calendar.

Once study groups are organized, I order supporting resources. I budget so that I can purchase study group materials in the spring for the following year. I purchase journals and books for each participant in the group. I always hand out the books to teachers before they leave for the summer. Many teachers like to read the book over the summer, and then reread it through the course of the study group. I order a few extra books for new teachers who ask to join the study group in September. If I end up with extra books, I put them in the literacy room. Extra resources enable staff who are not part of a study group to explore the books being used. If I have done my job organizing, the groups should be able to run smoothly without a lot of additional work from me.

Monthly study groups are scheduled for an hour. It's important that time be honored and the group end promptly. Teachers have places to go and kids to pick up at the end of the day. Although study groups end on time, I always hang out for a while for anyone who wants to stay and talk.

Figure 4.4

EFFECTIVE STRATEGIES FOR PROMOTING BOOK STUDY GROUPS

Getting Started

- Choose a focus for the group (book and/or video series).
- Seek volunteers who are interested in new learning.
- Limit the number of participants to eight people.
- Set meeting dates before starting the group.
- Order books and videos for participants.
- Organize resources for participants.
- Provide healthful snacks (vegetables, cheese, crackers) and chocolate, soda, and water.

Practical Tips for a Focus Group Session

- Limit sessions to one hour.
- Meet in a relaxed environment.
- Establish a predictable format for the session.
- Always honor ending time.
- Don't teach . . . this format promotes discovery through inquiry.
- Remember, participants have volunteered to be part of the group.

Many teachers stay to look through new resources displayed in the literacy room.

Most of the study groups are scheduled in the literacy room, but we also use conference rooms and the school libraries as alternative locations.

Establishing a Predictable Routine

Over the years the study groups have taken on a predictable routine. I use the same format for each study group, regardless of the topic. Teachers have shared that they like the predictability of the group. I have found that an hour session is an optimal amount of time for a meeting tacked on to an already-packed workday. A two-hour study group takes on more of an in-service feel. Study groups are broken into three components: whole-group discussion, viewing the videotape or reading the excerpt, and whole-group discussion—putting our ideas into practice.

Whole-Group Discussion (20 Minutes)

Each study group session starts with an open-ended whole-group discussion. Focus question sheets are always on the table for participants to take as they come in. I encourage participants to take a few minutes and jot down their thinking. Writing out thoughts helps keep the discussion focused. It also allows for less-verbal participants to process their thinking and have something in front of them to share.

Typical focus questions to start the meeting include the following:

- What are you thinking as a result of our last session?
- What is working well in your classroom?
- What are potential roadblocks to implementing change in your classroom?

Between sessions I encourage participants to read a chapter from our common text. Often our opening discussions are focused around new thinking from the text. We talk about ideas that we might try or strategies that we are using and agree are effective with students. Conversations around new thinking are encouraged, rather than the adoption of new activities. Our goal is not to "become" the teachers that we are exploring but to gain insight from their best practices in literacy.

Discussions are not always focused on the topic that we are exploring in the group. Recently in a study group using the resources *Still Learning to Read* and *Bringing Reading to Life* (videotape) by Franki Sibberson and Karen Syzmusiak, a new teacher said she was struggling with implementing literature circles based on the work of Harvey Daniels. This really had nothing to do with our text, but everything to do with her establishing a comprehensive literacy program in her classroom. The next fifteen minutes were spent with everyone sharing about how they implement literature circles in their own classrooms. What was so exciting about this was that *Literature Circles* by Harvey Daniels was the basis for the very first study group offered five years earlier. At the time, "literature circle" was a new concept for most of the teachers. Yet here we were five years later, with teachers confidently discussing how literature circles work in their room.

This example supports the research that change takes time, and that implementation of new learning is not always immediate (Fullan 1991). I realized that the practice of literature circles had become an integral part of these teachers' reading workshops. I hadn't seen the immediate results of that initial study group on literature circles five years before, but now was able to listen to the veteran teachers share the nuts and bolts of implementing literature discussion groups with a first-year teacher.

The discussion usually lasts about twenty minutes before we transition into the next part of the session. It's tempting to start the group with a video or jump into the meat of a book, but the open discussion is an essential part of the study group, because it provides teachers the time and opportunity to process their new thinking.

Viewing the Video or Reading a Book Excerpt (20 Minutes)

After the initial discussion we move into reading a book excerpt or viewing a video segment. We take about twenty minutes and read a few pages from our focus text. This is intended to whet the appetites of the participants in hopes that they will read more of the chapter on their own time. Throughout the course of the study group I select different excerpts for participants to read. I never go through a book chapter by chapter and expect teachers to read the whole book. The study group is not a course. My hope is that teachers will choose to read the book because they want to, not because it was "assigned."

During other meetings we will watch a video segment instead of reading. I have found video segments to be very effective. Teachers love catching a glimpse of other teachers in action. I focus the participants' viewing of the videos by providing them with a two-column journal entry (examples include Ideas You Might Want to Try/Obstacles That May Prevent

A study group in action.

A FEW CHOICE BOOKS AND COMPLEMENTARY VIDEOS

Book	Video
Reading with Meaning, Debbie Miller	*Happy Reading!,* Debbie Miller
I Read It, but I Don't Get It, Cris Tovani	*Thoughtful Reading,* Cris Tovani
Still Learning to Read, Franki Sibberson and Karen Szymusiak This group wanted more examples of explicit instruction so I used multiple video examples of authors with the same philosophy.	*Bringing Reading to Life,* Franki Sibberson and Karen Szymusiak *Happy Reading!,* Debbie Miller *Thoughtful Reading,* Cris Tovani
Word Savvy, Max Brand	*A Day with Words,* Max Brand *Focus on Spelling,* Diane Snowball
Strategies That Work, Stephanie Harvey and Anne Goudvis	*Strategy Instruction in Action,* Stephanie Harvey and Anne Goudvis
Craft Lessons, Ralph Fletcher and JoAnn Portalupi	*When Students Write,* Ralph Fletcher and JoAnn Portalupi *Talking About Writing,* JoAnn Portalupi and Ralph Fletcher

Figure 4.5

You from Trying, and Similarities to Your Classroom/Differences to Your Classroom).

Sometimes I pull in videos that are not directly related to the text we are reading. While working with *Still Learning to Read* and *Bringing Reading to Life* the teachers became interested in how Franki taught the concept of theme to her students. One of the teachers said theme was a difficult concept to teach fourth-grade students. I decided to share a segment from *Happy Reading!* by Debbie Miller. I wanted to show the group how Debbie introduced the concept of theme to her first-grade students and how similar strategies can be used with different grade levels.

Professional videos are great discussion starters. They are well worth the initial investment. Teachers have also shared that they like getting the opportunity to see how other teachers use their classroom space. Videos provide the visual links to instruction that are not always captured through professional books. Teachers often borrow the videos to rewatch segments for a second and third time.

Whole-Group Discussion: Putting Ideas into Practice (20 Minutes)

The last twenty minutes is another whole-group discussion sharing thoughts about the video, reading, and putting ideas into practice. After watching Debbie Miller in *Happy Reading!* teach theme to her first-grade students, the teachers decided they wanted to try teaching theme to their students. I copied and shared the graphic organizers from the video viewing guides that Franki and Debbie used in their classrooms.

A few other teachers had already begun reexamining how they taught theme and had worked up organizers that they had tried with students. All the organizers were shared with the group. The group decided that they would continue to try out these new strategies for teaching theme and share new learning and thoughts at our next meeting.

Figure 4.6

ESTABLISHING A PREDICTABLE FORMAT

- **Whole-Group Discussion**

If this is the start of a new study group, this time is spent reflecting on current practices and creating a learning community. During future meetings, this time is spent sharing new thinking and ideas that participants have tried.

- **Viewing the Video/Reading Excerpt**

This is an opportunity for the group to work with current research/resources around the chosen topic.

- **Whole-Group Discussion**

Participants share thoughts based on the video and reading excerpt.

- **Putting Ideas into Practice**

Decide on reading to be done between sessions. The reading is then used as a discussion starter. It is not expected that the group will read the book cover to cover. The intention of the reading excerpts from the book is to whet the appetite of the participants in hopes that they will dig deeper into the text on their own.

- **Follow-Up Between Sessions**

Remind participants of the next meeting and the materials they need to bring. Provide additional resources to help participants implement new ideas.

At the end of the session the group always decides on additional reading that they will do between sessions. Participants are encouraged to try something new in their classroom and bring samples of student work to the next session to share.

The study groups never adhere strictly to the outlined time frames. Sometimes the discussions go longer and we cut out the reading excerpt or the video segment. I always ask the group what they want to skip if we are short on time. The components all balance out in the end. Because this is a volunteer group, we don't need to fit it all in. We move along at a pace that works for the group.

Providing Additional Resources

I always budget extra funds for each study group. This money is used to purchase additional resources for teachers as needed. School budgets are often set a year in advance. When teachers want a new resource, they are often told to put it on their budget for the following year. Unfortunately by the time they are able to get the materials they wanted, the idea and passion for the change is long gone.

As teachers generate new ideas for their classrooms, I want to be able to help them make the change immediately. The resources teachers want usually do not cost a lot of money. When reading Cris Tovani's book *I Read It, but I Don't Get It,* teachers wanted additional sticky notes and highlighters so they could teach students various ways to hold their thinking. I was able to support this idea by buying Post-its and highlighters for the teachers in the study group. I have also bought plastic bins for teachers looking to redesign and organize their libraries. Teachers are appreciative of the additional support to help their ideas become reality.

Resources teachers have requested include the following:

- Highlighters
- Various sized Post-its
- Highlighting tape
- Folders
- Individual dry-erase boards for students
- Plastic bins
- Post-it flags
- Journals
- Magnetic letters
- Binders
- Plastic sheet protectors

What Teachers Say About Study Groups

At the end of each school year I ask teachers for feedback about their participation in the study groups. One teacher recently wrote,

> *The format allows for rich, focused conversations about best practice (and sometimes worst ☺). It also allows teachers to connect, reflect on, and redirect their teaching strategies. I have learned new strategies to revitalize and enrich read-alouds. I will also utilize the strategy of rereading as more of a way to promote thoughtful literature discussions. Although it happened by chance, the laughs and sweet food (along with productive conversations about literacy) have become a special part of my teaching experience. It's one that I always look forward to.*

Feedback as documented in the evaluations support the fact that teachers regard study groups as a highly effective model for professional development.

I use the teacher evaluations from the study groups as documentation of participation so that I can issue teachers contact hours for recertification. I also review teacher feedback to plan new study groups. Previous evaluations have communicated to me that teachers want to stay with the same group and topics for more than a year. They remind me that change takes time, so I shouldn't worry about always offering new topics. The administration recognizes study groups as an effective form of professional

Figure 4.7

SAMPLE OF STUDY GROUP EVALUATION

Thanks for participating in study groups this year. It is helpful to me to get feedback. I also need documentation so that we can continue to get funding to support teacher study groups. Thanks, Jen

1. What was the greatest benefit of participating in this type of professional development format?
2. What changes may you make in your instruction as a result of attending this focus group?
3. Please rate this form of professional development on a scale of 1 to 5 (5 being the highest).
4. Comments

TEACHER COMMENTS AND PLANS FOR CHANGE

Teacher Comments About Participation in Study Groups

- "Study groups provide me an opportunity to talk and share with my colleagues. We never seem to have time during the regular school day. Throughout the year, I feel the group breathes new life into teaching."
- "I rate study groups as the highest form of professional development."
- "Study groups provide me with the latest resources so that I can stay current on new literacy practices."
- "Thank you for organizing the study groups. The format honors teachers as being able to lead their own learning!"
- "I love hearing and seeing teaching ideas. Discussing ideas, sharing student products, and reading about theory that directly impacts my instruction fuels me as a learner and as a teacher. When I see a great idea, I may personalize it, but I've got to try it out. Idea sharing is passion sharing, and this translates as enthusiasm in the classroom."
- "Word Study—I want to have my kids 'deduct' more of their understanding from examining words in text. I'm planning on using the screening test in *Word Journeys* next year."
- "My classroom library will be set up differently—possibly my entire classroom. Can I make that huge step?"
- "In general I will be making the effort to regularly practice first what I ask my students to do as readers when I am reading myself."
- "Looking at what was most important to report about student achievement has allowed me to rethink what was most important in my day-to-day instruction. As I plan and instruct now, I feel more focused on the purpose of student learning."
- "I would like to do more with read-aloud. I am not sure how I want to change it. I am also thinking about the reading notebook."

Figure 4.8

development and provides financial support to purchase resources for the group. The evaluations are also used by the administration as documentation of the professional development activities that teachers participated in over the year. See Figure 4.8 for samples of teacher comments.

The feedback from teachers on study groups has been overwhelmingly positive. Almost all teachers who have participated have remained committed to the monthly study group sessions. Teachers have commented that they would like to see study group meetings offered during the allotted district in-service days. Right now teachers still attend study group meetings on their own time, but they receive recertification hours for study group participation. The administration values study groups as an effective form of professional development. One administrator said, "Study groups are vital for establishing professional collegiality among teachers. They create a culture of risk taking for learning."

A Worthy Investment

Study groups are what I am most passionate about as a literacy specialist. I believe in teachers and their ability to direct, reflect, and facilitate their own learning. I have seen firsthand how study groups drive new instructional practices in the classroom. In my experience, study groups are the most effective form of professional development for teachers. They require the smallest financial investment, yet yield the greatest return. Study groups provide participants with the opportunity to fulfill their professional cravings, and at the same time improve the quality of instruction delivered to students in the classroom.

At a recent state meeting of literacy specialists, several people said they thought they had great Title I programs. They went on to share the "programs" that were successful with their students receiving Title I. I reflected on their comments but thought to myself that I didn't really want a great Title I program. I wanted to improve the quality of instruction in all primary classrooms so that we didn't need "great" intervention programs. The research by Richard Allington supports the idea of investing in teachers. In *What Really Matters for Struggling Readers,* Allington writes,

> *The most powerful feature of schools, in terms of developing children as readers and writers, is the quality of classroom instruction. Effective schools are simply schools where there are more classrooms where high-quality reading and writing instruction is regularly available. No school with mediocre classroom instruction ever became effective just by adding a high-quality remedial or resource room program. For too long we have ignored this fundamental aspect of schooling. We have added more support programs, more instructional aides, more specialist teachers, and more computers and software programs, while ignoring the powerful evidence on the importance of high-quality classroom teaching. (p. 112)*

I often feel in the minority as I advocate for putting resources into teachers, not programs.

Study groups provide teachers the opportunities to direct their own learning. Carl Rogers's belief, as shared in *Freedom to Learn for the 80s*, is that the most significant learning comes when it is self-initiated. He writes

> *Significant learning has a quality of personal involvement—the whole person in both feeling and cognitive aspects being in the learning event. It is self-initiated. Even when the impetus or stimulus comes from the outside, the sense of discovery, of reaching out, of grasping and comprehending, comes from within. It is pervasive. It makes a difference in the behavior, the attitudes, perhaps even the personality of the learner. It is evaluated by the learner. She knows whether it is meeting her need, whether it leads toward what she wants to know, whether it illuminates the dark area of ignorance she is experiencing. The locus of evaluation, we might say, resides definitely in the learner. Its essence is meaning. When such learning takes place, the element of meaning to the learner is built into the whole experience. (1983, p. 20)*

In my role as literacy specialist, the extrinsic rewards can be few and far between. However, there is nothing more satisfying than excited teachers sharing with me their new thinking. I am as enthusiastic as they are when they show me samples of student learning. I want to help teachers renew their passion for teaching and learning. I find the sharing of new learning and thinking energizing. It is genuine and sincere, especially when it comes from the real "experts" of the school . . . the teachers.

CHAPTER FIVE

Helping Kids on the Bubble: The Literacy Intervention Classroom

A reading specialist who does not enter a fully fixed and defined role must be able to negotiate his or her own identity.

ALFRED TATUM

How the Literacy Intervention Rooms Came to Be

In May at the end of my first year in the position as literacy specialist, I was sitting at my desk staring at a page with sixty names on it. These were the names of children in grades 4 and 5 identified as reading below grade level. These were the children I would be expected to serve over the next year with only one educational technician to assist me. The students were spread across fourteen classrooms, with at least four students per classroom needing services, not including children identified as needing the special education program. I was looking for new ways to help students in the classroom, rather than developing a traditional Title I pullout model.

Like many literacy specialists, one of the responsibilities of my job is the coordination of Title IA support. It would have been easy to fix the tutor shortage by taking on a full caseload of students myself. However, if I had gone the route of tutor, I never would have been able to get into classrooms to support teacher instruction, let alone have enough time to design and lead study groups and other workshops for colleagues. Richard Allington writes about the correlation between student achievement and the delivery of high-quality instruction by expert teachers (2000). I wanted to focus on improving the quality of instruction that we were providing to *all* students. From the onset, I was committed to supporting teachers in their literacy instruction. My hope was that student achievement would improve if we focused more energy on supporting classroom instruction as opposed to putting all of our resources toward supporting individual students.

I was working with open-minded administrators, so I had the opportunity to carve out and identify my new role within the school. It was a chance to think differently about how the students' needs could be met.

Allington and his colleagues in their research demonstrate how students benefit from long, uninterrupted chunks of learning time, as well as consistent instruction from high-quality teachers (Allington 2000). Yet our neediest kids tend to have the most segmented days, being shuffled from "intervention" to "intervention." I'd always heard about the importance of helping "the lowest of the low"—those students who faced serious academic failure. Many of these students who would benefit from supplemental Title I support had a complex array of social, physical, or behavioral problems that would require support well beyond what I could provide alone.

Yet as I looked at the profiles of the sixty students, I realized that many of these kids were on the "bubble"—they were no more than a year or two below grade level. They weren't as needy or low performing as many students who were constantly the topics of meetings, interventions, and discussions among colleagues. They didn't have serious behavior problems, and many had been in Waterville schools since kindergarten. Yet for some reason, they were slowly falling behind their peers. Once they reached middle school, I feared there would be little hope of them catching up. I decided to work with teachers and administrators to develop a literacy intervention specifically tailored to the needs of these "bubble kids"—thus the intervention classroom was created. The hope was that if these targeted students got an extra learning boost, they would not require supplemental services in the long run.

Supporting Students on the Bubble Through Inclusive Support

We are identified as a Schoolwide Title I Program. This means we do not need to identify students who are "eligible" or "ineligible" for services— any student can receive additional support. We qualify for this flexibility

Figure 5.1

LITERACY INTERVENTION ROOM: KEY COMPONENTS

- Class size of 14 students
- Documentation of student achievement through portfolios
- Ongoing informal assessing to monitor individual student strengths and needs
- Breakdown and layering of instruction and curriculum
- Daily opportunities for students to talk through thinking
- Visual models for students to reference
- Large blocks of uninterrupted literacy instruction
- Explicit fluency instruction with student self-monitoring
- Daily reading and writing workshops (working to increase volume)
- Multiple opportunities for students to be reading at their instructional and independent reading level
- Explicit daily writing instruction within workshop model
- Graphic organizers used throughout in all academic areas
- Highly structured and predictable routine
- Integration of literacy throughout the content areas
- Classroom library filled with new and readable titles
- High classroom expectations
- Student involvement in activities outside the classroom (e.g., student council, newspaper, civil rights committee)
- Student responsibilities in the classroom: class meetings, weekly jobs

of programming through Title IA because of our high poverty rate as determined by the percentage of students who receive free and reduced-price lunches (almost 56 percent).

As the result of our tutoring predicament and the district's renewed commitment to improving the quality of literacy instruction within our schools, the intervention classroom was created for students on the bubble of literacy success. I worked with the principal, Harriet Trafford, to create two specialized classrooms (one at grade 4 and the other at grade 5) that would service students within an inclusive setting, provide large uninterrupted blocks of time, and provide students with an extra jolt of literacy instruction. We created the fourth-grade intervention room the first year and the fifth-grade intervention classroom the following year. During the second year, the students from the fourth-grade intervention room moved on to a newly designed fifth-grade intervention room. We wanted them to have two years of continual support. These classrooms, of fourteen students each, taught students through an integrated curriculum that provided practice and repetition of concepts taught for students to demonstrate fluency and automaticity for concepts learned.

Curt Dudley-Marling and Patricia Paugh write, "The only way to address the needs of struggling readers successfully is by creating classroom structures that enable teachers to do ongoing assessments and provide students with frequent, intensive, explicit, and individualized support and direction as needed without adding to the already overwhelming demands of teachers" (2004, p. ix). Harriet and I knew we needed to look at the actual classroom schedule of this fourth-grade intervention classroom. In looking at the master schedule for the school Harriet made sure that the classroom had large blocks of uninterrupted time and tried to schedule art, music, physical education, and library at consistent times across the week so that daily routines could be maintained.

From the initial conception of the literacy classroom we knew students would work within an inclusive setting with the same teacher for the entire day. Students would not be pulled out for any supplemental support. I would provide support by going into the classrooms and working alongside the selected classroom teachers.

Research by James Gee suggests that unlike riding a bike, which once mastered is maintained, struggling readers never learn to read "once and for all" (Dudley-Marling and Paugh 2004). The intent of the intervention rooms was never to "cure" the students of reading difficulties. Rather, we wanted to provide them with the individualized support and strategies that would help them experience success and gain academic self-confidence. We wanted to support these students on the bubble as long as we could.

Harriet and I pitched the newly designed classroom, with plans to expand to fifth grade the following year, to the assistant superintendent. He was excited about this innovation because the program was based on a need, designed around best practice, and yearly evaluation of the program was planned. We shared that students would be assessed in literacy in both fall and spring.

Continuation of the program beyond the first year would hinge on student achievement. We promised to monitor student progress and report our data to the school board at the end of the first year.

Selling the Concept of an Intervention Room to the Staff

The next step was to sell the concept of the intervention room to the staff. We shared the concept of the intervention room at a staff meeting. I antic-

"THE VISION" DISTRIBUTED TO THE SCHOOL COMMUNITY: THE LITERACY CLASS

Vision

This classroom is designed to accelerate student achievement and to provide students with the tools needed to make them more strategic learners, so that they will experience success in all curriculum areas.

Goals

- Communicate effectively through oral and written language
- Transfer and apply literacy knowledge to real-life applications
- Access information in all content areas
- Complete assigned tasks using study skills and organizational strategies
- Work independently
- Develop independent problem solving skills

Research

- Children need to read a great deal (volume) to become proficient readers (Allington 2001; Krashen 2004).
- Children need access to appropriate books and instructional materials (Allington 2001).
- Strategy instruction enhances reading comprehension (Harvey and Goudvis 2000).
- Children need to develop fluent reading to become proficient readers (Rasinski 2003).
- Children struggling in literacy need instruction that is intensive, explicit, and individualized (Dudley-Marling and Paugh 2004).

The Literacy Classroom

This classroom will serve selected students identified as "on the bubble" for literacy success. These students would benefit from a strategic approach to literacy instruction delivered within a small-group setting.

This class will serve no more than fourteen students. Research shows greater student achievement when students are placed in small classes with expert teachers.

The classroom structures will be predictable and consistent. Students will be immersed in strategy instruction that will support learning in all content areas. Students will specifically be taught strategies to help them build reading stamina and fluency so that they will become more proficient readers and writers.

Students will receive direct instruction in the areas of reading, word study, and writing. Students will learn study skills and organizational strategies. Students will be taught strategies for short-term and long-term planning.

continued

Figure 5.2

Students will be engaged in literacy within a workshop approach to teaching. Students will participate in daily guided literature groups, writer's workshop (independent and guided writing), word study, independent reading, and read-aloud. Instructional methods will be both direct and indirect. Students will also be provided with opportunities to learn through inquiry. Skills will be embedded within a rich literacy program using a variety of texts and genres matched to readers' interests and abilities.

There will be experiences for building skills necessary for success in junior high school. Attention will be given to informational and textbook reading strategies. Students will be taught how to use informational parts of nonfiction texts to enhance their understanding of the text, identify nonfiction text structures, and determine important information. Students will learn how to layer texts as a strategy to support fluency and build background knowledge for textbook reading in the content areas.

Graphic organizers will be used within the classroom as tools to help students organize and apply their thinking within all content areas. Instruction will be tailored to meet students' individual needs.

Parent Link

Parents will be expected to support students by making sure their child has regular attendance. It is expected that parents will participate in the home reading program.

Figure 5.2
continued

ipated that teachers might be resistant to the idea because maintaining the intervention room class size of fourteen students meant that each of the regular classrooms would need to absorb one to two more students. I was pleasantly surprised by the staff's overwhelming support of the classroom. The teachers knew that our struggling reading population was growing. They also acknowledged that they did not think they had the skills to meet the needs of this group at the intermediate level. An intervention room could help absorb some of the students needing extra assistance in literacy.

Selecting Teachers

The key to the success of the literacy intervention classroom would be the teacher. Research shows that the best teachers produce the students who progress the most (Dole 2004). The teacher selected for the classroom needed a strong background in literacy instruction and in using assessment to guide instruction. Harriet and I established criteria to help select the best candidate for the job, and the position was advertised in-house. See Figure 5.3 for the criteria we used.

TEACHER CRITERIA FOR SELECTION

- Background in assessment and evaluation (document relevant course work/workshops)
- Demonstrates use of multiple methods of ongoing informal assessments used in the classroom to inform instruction and document student achievement (informal reading assessments, miscue analysis, writing prompts, developmental spelling inventories, and portfolios)
- Solid understanding of the reading process (understanding decoding and comprehension)
- Background and familiarity in teaching reading through reading workshop approach (familiarity with the work of Regie Routman, Janet Allen, Lucy Calkins, Cris Tovani, Franki Sibberson, and Karen Szymusiak)
- Background in teaching explicit reading comprehension strategies (familiarity with the work of Stephanie Harvey and Anne Goudvis)
- Background in and familiarity with teaching writing through a writer's workshop approach (familiarity with the work of Donald Graves, Lucy Calkins, Ralph Fletcher and JoAnn Portalupi)
- Background knowledge of and familiarity with implementation of student literature discussions (familiarity with the work of Harvey Daniels)
- Background knowledge of and familiarity with incorporating word study throughout the day (understanding of the interrelationship of sound, patterns, and meanings of words)
- Demonstrated how graphic organizers would be incorporated into instruction
- Familiarity with fourth-grade curriculum expectations and state educational assessments administered at grade 4
- Background in strategies-based teaching
- Strong classroom management techniques as supported in previous classroom observations
- Demonstrated ability to maintain predictable daily schedule and routines

Figure 5.3

Interested teachers were interviewed. Carolyn Bridges was selected the first year to teach the newly created fourth-grade literacy intervention room. She had three years of teaching experience and a master's degree in education, with strength in literacy and assessment. Carolyn was also familiar with the latest research on struggling readers. She had already demonstrated her ability as a teacher to run a well-organized classroom while implementing daily reading and writing workshops.

Lesley Fowler was hired to teach the fifth-grade literacy intervention room, which would start the following year. She was licensed as a literacy specialist, a gifted and talented teacher, music teacher, and certified in English Language Learning. Lesley had more than twenty years' teaching experience. She had a background in assessment and knew all the latest research on struggling readers. Like Carolyn, she demonstrated that she was a lifelong learner and had a zest for life. Lesley was well known for teaching students to knit and providing piano lessons.

Selecting Students for the Intervention Classroom

A list of student criteria was developed to guide classroom teachers in recommending students for the literacy intervention classroom. Student selec-

Figure 5.4

STUDENT CRITERIA FOR INTERVENTION CLASSROOM

- **Typically not served in special education**—There are other services in our school for these children, and their needs are often more varied.
- **One grade level behind in reading and writing**—Kids on the bubble are almost at grade level. By third grade, children who are reading at the second-grade level have mastered most decoding skills. But they lack fluency and basic reading comprehension skills.
- **Not transient**—We wanted to service children who had been in our system since kindergarten. We were fairly confident of the quality and consistency of the literacy instruction students received in our school district throughout the primary grades. We knew the regular literacy program was not working for these children.
- **Excellent attendance**—The intervention classrooms would be built on predictable routines, with day-to-day scaffolding of instruction. If children were missing a lot of school, much of the teacher's time would be spent helping them catch up on work they had missed. Group interventions also rely on forming a cohesive community, which won't happen for children who are frequently absent.
- **Socioeconomic mix that matches that of the school**—Approximately 56 percent of the students in our district receive free or reduced-price lunch. We also have a strong population of children who come from upper-middle-class homes—many of these students have parents who are doctors, lawyers, or professors associated with the elite private college in our community. It was important to us to have a socioeconomic mix in the intervention program that matched that of the community. We didn't want the program to appear to isolate and stigmatize students from low-income families. We found in the data that struggles with literacy were more common in the free and reduced-price lunch population, but there were still many children from wealthier, stable families who were falling behind.
- **No major guidance or behavior issues**—Over the past few years, we have seen a tremendous growth in our community in the number of students and adults who need special services for mental illnesses. We wanted to separate these needs from academic struggles, to best use our academic resource base for academic needs.

tion was a thoughtful and timely process. We began the selection process in March. Grade 3 teachers, the school principal, and the guidance counselor were asked to recommend students they thought would benefit from the classroom and fit the criteria that we established. We always referred to the criteria list as we made the tough decisions about student placement in the program. See Figure 5.4 for the student criteria we used.

Moving Beyond Student Names to Looking at Each Student

After asking for student recommendations for this classroom, we were faced with a long list of potential candidates for the intervention room. Carolyn worked with me, combing through student cumulative folders, talking with classroom teachers, and, most important, observing the students in their classroom setting. We wanted to put a face to each name we had on paper. We observed all candidates in their classrooms and made additional notes. We compiled the information on a profile sheet for each student. It was at this point that Carolyn; Harriet, the principal at the school; and I sat down with the list of student names and student profile sheets to make final selections for the class. See Figure 5.5 for a student profile form and Figure 5.6 for a completed sheet.

In addition to these criteria, I was looking for students who had demonstrated some level of *intrinsic motivation* for their own learning. I asked classroom teachers to consider the following question in addition to the outlined student criteria: "Who are the kids who are intrinsically motivated and whom you think could be anything they wanted to be in life, yet are continually struggling to meet literacy expectations?" It was this final subjective question that helped us weed through the list of students who had been recommended for the literacy intervention classroom.

Working with Parents

Final selections for the intervention classroom were determined by the end of March. The next key piece was to get parent support for the program. We wanted parents to understand the philosophy of the literacy intervention room and to support their child's placement in the room. We asked that grade 3 teachers make the first contact with families to explain the program. We thought this was a logical route because the classroom teachers had already established relationships with the student and parents. Once the classroom teachers explained the program, they invited the par-

Figure 5.5

STUDENT PROFILE SHEET
LITERACY INTERVENTION ROOM, GRADE 4

Student:

Date of Entry:
- History of Interventions:
- Independent Reading Level _____
  Strengths:
  Needs:
- Independent Writing Level _____
  Strengths:
  Needs:
- Independent Spelling Level _____
  Strengths:
  Needs:
- Completes Tasks Independently in the Classroom:
  Does Not Meet _____ Partially Meets _____ Meets _____ Exceeds _____
- Completes Homework:
  Does Not Meet _____ Partially Meets _____ Meets _____ Exceeds _____
- Teacher Comments:
- Guidance Comments:

ents to meet with Carolyn. Carolyn was given a release day to meet one-on-one with parents of the recommended students. It was during this meeting that parents learned more about the classroom and accepted or declined the invitation to have their child participate. In four years of implementing this program only three parents have declined the invitation.

Summer Literacy Jump Start

Students entering the literacy intervention rooms were invited to participate in our Summer Literacy Jump Start. The purpose of this program is to get students back into the school and acclimated to the classroom as they begin their immersion into literacy. Carolyn and Lesley each invited their class to school the week before the school year started. Summer Literacy Jump Start ran for four days before the start of school, for two hours each morning. Carolyn and Lesley each ran their own class. This was a time to

Figure 5.6
A completed
student profile.

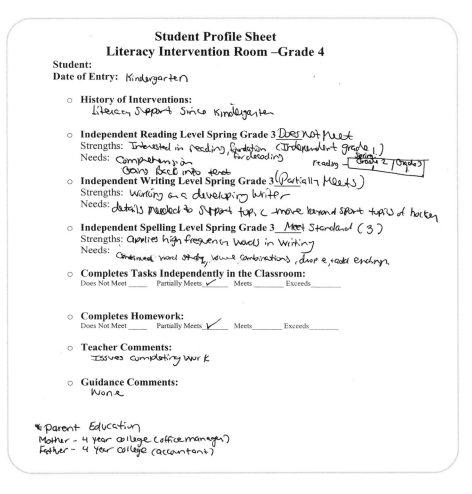

get to know one another, start building a classroom community, and ease the beginning-of-school anxieties. Games of four-square, sharing snacks at break, listening to stories read aloud, and relating our summer adventures helped the children relax and look forward to returning to school. Carolyn and Lesley also provided school supplies for students who needed them, another opportunity for them to start building relationships with both the students and parents.

The morning was broken into three parts: reading, snack and chat, and writing snapshots. They began each day by sharing a favorite new picture book. The purpose was for students to see Carolyn's and Lesley's love for reading and books and to start getting them interested and hooked on reading. They spent the week reading and getting students to talk about books, with a focus on listening and speaking. Students also spent time

SUMMER LITERACY JUMP START SCHEDULE

	Monday	Tuesday	Wednesday	Thursday
Reading **8:30–9:15**	Picture Book Read-Aloud Strategies for Book Selection	Picture Book Read-Aloud Strategies for Book Selection	Picture Book Read-Aloud Strategies for Book Selection	Field Trip to Local Bookstore
Community **Building** **9:15–9:30**	Snack/Chat	Snack/Chat	Snack/Chat	Snack/Chat
Writing **9:30–10:30**	Students Given Writer's Notebooks; Introduced to Snapshot Writing	Snapshot Writing	Snapshot Writing	Independent Reading of New Books Snapshot Writing

Figure 5.7

exploring the classroom library. Summer Literacy Jump Start was an added opportunity to get students excited about books and whet their appetites for reading.

Carolyn and Lesley worked to establish a safe environment where students could get to know each other before academic demands were placed on them. Both teachers went to great lengths to get to know each student—his favorite ice cream, her passion for dancing. The week was designed to ease school anxieties for students; these were the students who were used to hearing that they were "almost there" but that what they produced was never quite good enough.

Carolyn and Lesley also started the students writing. They purchased a variety of fancy journals and let the children select their own writer's notebook. Some chose candy striped, whereas others went for a gilt-edged journal. The week was devoted to introducing students to snapshot writing. This gave them a chance to tell their stories through short pieces of text and to celebrate their stories. The intention was for students to feel comfortable and confident as writers.

The culmination of the week was a field trip to a local bookstore. Teachers spent time each day teaching students book selection strategies and how to find just the right book. Students then got to apply these strategies when they were at the bookstore. Each student selected a book to take home. This was the highlight of the week. Students were thrilled that they could actually keep the book. Figure 5.7 shows the program schedule.

Summer Literacy Jump Start has continued each summer before the start of the school year. Students entering the fourth- and fifth-grade literacy intervention rooms are invited to participate in the summer session. Funding for the week is provided through Title I money. This money pays for supplies, snacks, books, teacher salaries, and transportation. Summer Literacy Jump Start has proven to be a successful experience for the students, parents, and teachers involved.

Figure 5.8

RESEARCH PRINCIPLES FOR THE LITERACY ROOM

Research Says . . .	How Literacy Classroom Supports Research
Volume and time engaged in reading correlates to reading achievement (Allington 2001; Krashen 2004).	Students are actively engaged in reading. Students participate in daily reading workshop and independent reading.
Students need access to books appropriate to their ability and interests (Allington 2001).	Series books are used as a vehicle to hook students on reading. Series books appeal to student interests and match reading ability.
Strategy instruction enhances reading comprehension (Harvey and Goudvis 2000).	Students are taught strategies to find evidence in the text to support their thinking while reading. Students are provided tools (Post-its, graphic organizers, highlighters) to hold and organize their thinking.
Students need to develop fluency to become proficient readers (Rasinski 2003).	Students are provided daily opportunities to read and reread books at their independent and instructional levels.
Struggling readers need instruction that is intensive, explicit, and individualized (Dudley-Marling and Paugh 2004).	Instruction is tailored to meet the individual needs of the students.

DIFFERENCES BETWEEN REGULAR CLASSROOMS AND LITERACY INTERVENTION ROOMS

	Regular Classroom	Literacy Intervention Room
Class Size	Class size 20–23 students.	Reduced class size of 14 students.
Multiple Teachers	Students switch teachers for math, science, and social studies.	Inclusive setting; teacher teaches all subjects to students.
Delivery of Services	Pull-out services—Students are pulled out for special education services.	Pull-in services—Supplemental support is provided in the format of the literacy specialist working in the classroom in collaboration with the classroom teacher. All students are targeted and supported.
Scheduling Time with Whole Class	Students come and go throughout the day from classroom for services.	Teacher has the whole class for the entire day and does not have to worry about re-teaching lessons.
Daily Schedule	Daily schedules are created around pull-out specials of art, music, and physical education. Literacy blocks are scheduled around special education availability. Literacy blocks are designated throughout the day from morning through end of day.	Consistent, predictable, daily schedule created around large uninterrupted blocks of time designated for morning literacy instruction.
Mobility	High mobility rate—students moving in and out during the year.	Because students are selected based on the criteria of long-term residence, very few students move. Students are not placed in the literacy room during the year.

Figure 5.9

Starting the Year: Establishing Predictable Routines

Dudley-Marling and Paugh point out that all learners, including struggling readers, need predictable, well-ordered learning environments (2004). The intervention classroom schedules were highly predictable. Carolyn and

Lesley embedded organizational tools within the day to support students as they accessed and applied new learning. These routines and structures were taught to the students starting the first day they entered the classrooms. One of the goals of the rooms was to have students become independent learners. Students were taught how to organize their work in folders and notebooks. They were then held accountable for writing down nightly assignments and completing homework expectations. Carolyn and Lesley held their students to the highest standards and were thrilled when they rose to meet their expectations.

Boot Camp: First Month of Training

The first month of school is what we called our Literacy Boot Camp. We spent the first month of school training students in the tools they would be using during reading workshop. We knew that if students were clear on the expectations during reading workshop, they would be better prepared to work independently when we moved to small literature groups. Graphic organizers were one of the tools that we taught students to use to hold and access their thinking.

Through past teaching experience, I had found that students spent a great deal of time trying to figure out the different graphic organizers teachers gave them. We wanted to invest upfront in making sure students clearly understood how to fill out the organizers and how they could support their learning. Carolyn, Lesley, and I selected a handful of organizers that we could use throughout the year and across content areas. There are a million different graphic organizers out there for plotting character traits. All achieve the same outcome; they just look different. Differences in the layouts of graphic organizers can throw students off. Sticky notes were used to hold student thinking and later to arrange their thoughts on organizers. Opting for simplicity and consistency, we slowed down the start of the year and took the time to teach the whole class our expectations for strategic reading and how to hold and organize thinking using graphic organizers.

In both Carolyn's and Lesley's room, we started off with whole-class literature investigations. Carolyn's room ventured into an author study on Chris Van Allsburg, and Lesley explored the topic of the *Titanic* with her students. In both classes the focus was on listening and talking and books. The goal was to teach students to read deeply for various purposes and to use the various tools such as graphic organizers to hold and organize their thinking. The organizers introduced were the ones we would be using throughout both years. During the two-year program, each student would use the same simple graphic organizers for researching, planning, and writing a research paper. We also modeled and taught students strategies and expectations for writing responses to literature. They then practiced using the organizers and writing reading responses, applying them to the Chris Van Allsburg and *Titanic* books.

Fall Assessments to Inform Instruction

In the fall, students were administered assessments so that we could set instructional goals for them and tailor instruction to meet their individual needs. Each student was administered a Developmental Reading Assessment (DRA), writing prompt, constructed response, and the Developmental Spelling Assessment (created by Kathy Ganske). The information from these assessments provided us with baseline information and the needed insights into the strengths and needs of each child.

We continued to use informal assessments throughout the year to track student progress and to inform instruction. Student portfolios were created to document learning. Portfolios were organized by subject and contained student work samples from each trimester (see Figure 5.10). The portfolios

Figure 5.10

CONTENTS OF STUDENT PORTFOLIO ORGANIZED BY TRIMESTER

Reading	Math
• Student self-reflection	• Student self-reflection
• Copy of page from literature book identifying strategy student has been working on	• Multitask problem
	• Math facts
• Reading response	
• Fluency assessment	**Science/Social Studies**
	• Student self-reflection
	• Science investigation or social studies exploration
Writing	
• Student self-reflection	
• Copy of student writing from writing workshop (drafts and final product)	**Future Goals**
	• Student set goals for each content area
• Writing prompt	

were also used during parent/teacher conferences. Students were formally assessed again in the spring using the same assessments that had been administered in the fall (DRA, writing prompt, constructed response, and Developmental Spelling Assessment). Spring assessments were administered for the purpose of evaluating the success of the literacy intervention rooms.

Immersed in Literacy

Students read daily for different purposes. They were provided daily opportunities to read at both their independent and instructional level. Both classrooms were filled with books that would appeal to the students. We especially looked for new series books for Carolyn's room that might hook a student for several books. We wanted students reading lots of books at their independent level to improve their reading fluency and to increase their stamina for extended text. We also wanted to get students hooked on reading! Carolyn and Lesley expected students to use evidence from texts to support their thinking. Both classrooms used common graphic organizers to hold their thinking.

Graphic Organizers Common to Both Classrooms
Character Web
Story Maps
FQR—Facts/Questions/Response
Note-Taking Organizer
Research Organizer

Students wrote literature responses to the books they read. The biggest jump from fourth to fifth grade was moving these students out of kid-grabbing series books into more literature-rich books. By the end of fifth grade, students were reading with fluency and stamina books by Gary Paulsen, Kate DiCamillo, and Sharon Creech. Lesley was able to move students out of their comfort zone of series books and introduce students to new genres and challenges.

Breaking Down and Chunking Out Instruction

We also broke down the way we delivered instruction. Instead of passing out a character web and asking them to fill the whole web using evidence from the text to support their thinking, we asked students to fill out the first part of the web that asked them what the character liked. After fifteen minutes we came back as a class and shared our thinking, charting our evidence before moving on to the next section of the web. This strategy ensured that students understood what was being asked of them. It also kept them engaged in their learning, as they thumbed through and quickly learned that they couldn't wait us out and sit for forty-five minutes doing nothing. We gradually moved to having students work independently for larger chunks of time as we went through the school year. But we continued with the concept of breaking down instruction into chunks.

A Snapshot of One Morning in the Literacy Intervention Classrooms: Working with Students Through the Process of Research

Wednesday Morning—Carolyn's Room

With these newly designed classrooms I provide inclusive support (forty-five minutes, three times a week). I start my day each morning in Carolyn's intervention fourth-grade classroom with coffee in hand. On this day, after weeks of gathering information, students were going to start writing biographies of famous people. Our plan for the morning was to have them write the childhood section of their biography. That's all.

I was a bit apprehensive about starting the actual writing, because students had struggled through the process of identifying important supporting details to include in their biographies. We had spent the last three days working with them, helping them reread their notes and select supporting details to include in their writing. We also worked with students to help them organize and sequence the details onto a graphic organizer that they would then use as a road map for writing their papers.

I walked around the room as students organized their writing materials. I noticed that one student, Mark, had a whole page of notes on Albert Einstein's childhood. He had highlighted his thinking that Einstein was a strange boy who didn't like to play with other kids and did not like sports. Mark supported his thinking by sharing that he couldn't understand anyone not loving sports. Mark starts his morning in school by reading through the sports page of the newspaper!

I asked Mark if he would model his thinking in front of the class with me. He agreed to do so, and to write his section on childhood. Students are

Carolyn and I
confer with
students.

comfortable with the practice of talking through their thinking in front of the class, a strategy both Carolyn and Lesley use on a daily basis. I knew Mark had already chosen strong supporting details for his section on childhood and had a strong idea for his lead. Now was the time to pull his notes together and start to bring Albert Einstein alive as a child—or so we hoped. Mark shared his notes on Einstein's childhood with the class. He talked through his process of selecting the details he would include in his writing. Mark stuck with the notion that Einstein was strange. He wrote, "Albert Einstein was a strange boy!" Using his notes and graphic organizer, Mark wrote his section on Einstein's childhood. It was not extensive, but was solid and stuck to the main idea and central theme of Einstein being an eccentric child.

> *Albert Einstein was a strange boy. He didn't like to play sports or play with other kids. He couldn't tie his own shoes. Albert didn't like long sleeve shirts. He even hated school. I wonder if he had a lot of friends?*

The other students were engaged and interested in learning more about Albert Einstein. Mark had done a super job of talking through his process with the class. His writing reflected thoughtful consideration of a lead sen-

Carolyn and I
compile lead
sentences for
student
biographies in a
mini-lesson.

tence that would grab his audience. Most important, he captured Albert Einstein's personality as a young child.

Students started writing their sections on their subjects' childhoods, using their notes outlined on the graphic organizer. Carolyn and I circulated among the class, listening as they explained their writing plans to us. We periodically stopped the class to have students share their thinking and writing aloud with their peers.

We ended the writing workshop by asking students to share their lead sentences. Carolyn charted them on the overhead for others to see. It was a good place to stop and pick up the next day. We asked students to take a moment to read through all the lead sentences charted on the board and asked them, "Which lead sentences grab you enough that you want to read on about the person's childhood?"

Examples of lead sentences students shared included these:

- Thomas Edison was a curious child.
- Frederick Douglass had a difficult childhood.
- Did you know Harriet Tubman was born a slave?
- Do you know that Thomas Edison started his own laboratory as a kid?
- Amelia Earhart was known as a tomboy.
- There are many interesting facts about George Eastman's childhood.
- Albert Einstein asked a lot of questions as a child.

More Research—Lesley's Room

It was 9:15, and my coffee was now cold as I moved into Lesley's room. Books and papers were scattered everywhere. Students were already immersed in their individual research projects. They barely glanced up as I entered the room. I couldn't help but think back to the previous year, when they were the students struggling through their biography projects with Carolyn and me in fourth grade. These were the same students who had written lead sentences such as, "Hank Aaron was born on February 5, 1934." I was in complete awe of the research strategies these fifth-grade students were using only a year later. Books were piled high on desks. Students were pursuing learning to fulfill their own personal interests. What started out as an assignment turned into personal quests to become experts on their own topics. This is the learning that Carolyn and Lesley strive for with their students. It just takes time to see the payoff of what can happen when learning is broken down and layered over time. Carolyn lays the foundation during fourth grade, and Lesley is able to start the building process in fifth grade with the foundation that Carolyn has laid.

On this morning, students were reading through headings and thinking about a vision for their overall paper and how it might be organized.

Students work throughout the room compiling notes and referring to nonfiction resources.

Lesley had handed out transparencies to each student and asked them to write headings in the order that they were going to write about them.

Students had spent the last three weeks pursuing questions and topic headings of interest. They had taken copious notes on their topics, and it was time for them to think about their overall paper and their audience. It was also a time for students to see if they had gathered enough information on a heading or needed to go back and take more notes. It was an opportunity to ditch headings that were of little interest. Lesley had emphasized that research was not a linear process. Students were encouraged to rethink their questions and the topic headings on which they were gathering information.

I sat next to David and listened as he began to talk about Mount Everest. I was in awe of his knowledge base. He immediately began to rattle off fascinating facts about Mount Everest. I also couldn't believe this was the same student who wanted to write only about hockey in fourth grade. David took out his pile of note-taking organizers and read through his topic headings to me.

- Where is Mount Everest?
- What year were there the most deaths?
- What made the Khumba Glacier?
- Why were people chicken of climbing Everest?

I asked David if he had enough information using these topic headings to write a research paper. He replied, "My paper would be, like, four sentences if I only used these headings." I could sense his frustration, but at the same time knew that he had a wealth of information on Everest because he had just shared his new knowledge with me. It was the simple question, "Do you have enough information written on your note-taking organizers to write a research paper?" that got David rethinking the information he should present to his reader. Right away he said that he could write about the dangers on Mount Everest—if he did this, he could consolidate three of his current headings. I left David for a little while. When I returned, he had reworked his headings, gotten new note-taking organizers (the same blank note-taking organizers that had been used in fourth grade), and rewritten and reorganized his notes. David had also written his new topic headings on the transparency, as Lesley had asked. David read his new topic headings to me:

- Hillary and Norgay's Adventures
- Interesting Facts About Everest

- Dangers of Everest
- Everest Today

Wow! I was impressed with his thinking and revisions as the result of a few probing questions. Lesley asked David to share his overhead in front of the class and talk through his revisions and consolidation of headings and why he had changed his focus at this point in the process. As David stood in front of his peers, his classmates were mesmerized by his wealth of fascinating information on Mount Everest and his ability to articulate his thinking about his paper. It was amazing to see how many students raised their hands to ask David more probing questions about his topic out of sheer interest. It was 10:00 A.M. already and time for a break. Tomorrow we would continue to have students comb back through their notes and topic headings. We wanted them to keep thinking about their overall papers and audiences as they continued to refine and restructure the headings that they wanted for their final research papers. So far we had spent the last three weeks in Lesley's room reading, thinking, taking notes, and talking about the topics the students had chosen to study. This was time well spent, dedicated to having students build background knowledge and becoming experts on their topics, all before having them start writing their research papers. Figure 5.11 lays out the process in more detail.

Evaluating the Success of the Program: A Snapshot of Students Who Completed the Two-Year Intervention

Background Data

The students selected for the literacy classroom were working below grade-level expectations in reading and/or writing at the end of third grade. Fourteen students were part of the classroom at the start of fourth grade, but only thirteen students participated for the full two years. One student moved, and we added another student to the fifth-grade room to take his place. Twelve of the students had been enrolled in the school system since kindergarten or first grade. This classroom comprised seven boys and seven girls.

Reading Achievement

Students were formally assessed in the spring to determine growth in the area of literacy by taking the Developmental Reading Assessment (DRA), a tool that assesses reading engagement, fluency, and comprehension.

LAYERING OF RESEARCH STRATEGIES OVER TWO YEARS

The research approach is based on repetition, consistency, and the simplicity of layering readable text. Research strategies are reinforced over the two years.

Carolyn's Fourth-Grade Classroom	Lesley's Fifth-Grade Classroom
Carolyn began teaching research strategies in January and continued through May.	Lesley's class completed one research exploration per trimester.
January	**September**
Read Biographies	Whole-Class Exploration on the *Titanic*
• Direct instruction on how to use informational text features	• Reviewed strategies for determining important information
• Determined important information	• Reviewed note-taking graphic organizer
February	• Continued strategy of layering texts by
Wrote an Autobiography	readability (independent to instructional)
• Introduced note-taking and research graphic organizer	as a method to build background knowledge
March	**January**
Researched and Wrote a Biography	Independent Research Project
• Students were given guided practice and applied strategies learned	• Teacher provided guided practice and students applied strategies learned
• Began layering informational text resources on foundational resource	• Students practiced strategy of identifying text difficulty and finding resources to layer around their topic
April/May	**April/May**
Independent Research Project (Local Assessment)	Independent Research Project (Local Assessment)
• Independently researched topic, applied research strategies, and used organizers	• Independently applied and used research strategies and graphic organizers

Figure 5.11

In the spring of fourth grade 71 percent of the students met and/or exceeded the grade-level expectations for reading. All fourteen of the students made at least one year's growth, with five students making two years' growth in reading. Between the summer of fourth and fifth grade, all the students maintained their gains in reading with the exception of two who regressed.

Figure 5.12
Reading Gains

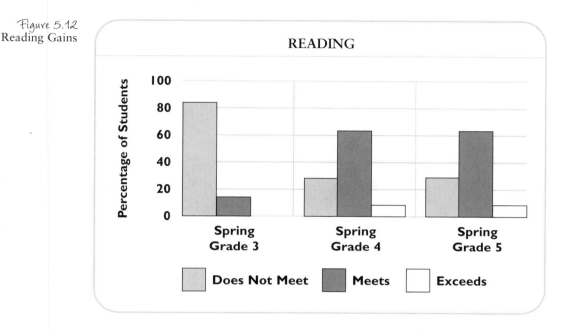

In the spring of fifth grade students were formally assessed again, using the DRA. At the end fifth grade all but four of the students met or exceeded the standard for end-of-year reading expectations. The four students who did not meet the standard continued to work one year below grade-level expectations. At the end of fifth grade 71 percent of the students met and/or exceeded the standard in reading compared with 59 percent of the school's fifth-grade class. See Figure 5.12.

Writing Achievement

Students were also assessed in writing via a writing prompt following the Maine Educational Assessment (MEA) scoring procedures.

At the end of third grade, none of the fourteen students met the standard for grade-level expectations in writing. By the spring of fourth grade seven of the students (50 percent) still did not meet the standard. However, six of the students (43 percent) shifted to partially meeting grade-level expectations, and one student met grade-level expectations for writing.

Students continued to make gains in writing during fifth grade (see Figure 5.13). The end-of-year writing assessment indicated that only two (14 percent) still did not meet the standard in writing. Ten of the students partially met the standard (72 percent). Only 40 percent of the school's fifth-grade class partially met the standard for writing, with the majority

Figure 5.13
Writing Gains

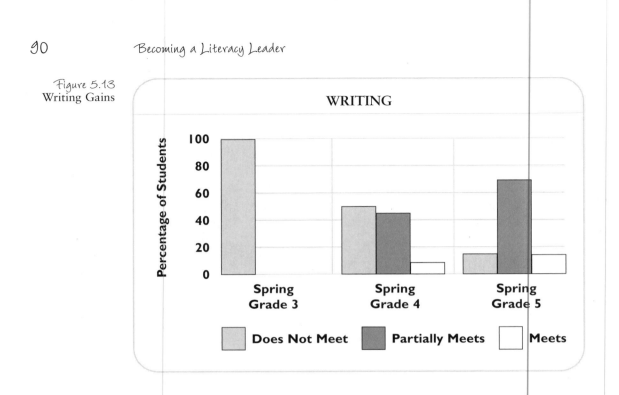

falling in the does-not-meet category. Two of the students demonstrated that they met the grade-level expectations for writing. This represents 14 percent of the class compared with 12 percent of the school's fifth-grade class that met the standard.

Student Survey

At the end of the year both fourth- and fifth-grade students were given a survey asking them to reflect on themselves as learners. It was exciting to see that 79 percent of the students recognized that they felt good or positive about themselves as learners. A total of 72 percent identified that reading and/or writing went well for them that year, and that they were making gains in literacy. One student wrote on the survey, "I became a better thinker." A fifth-grade student wrote, "I learned more this year than any other year." When asked the best part about school, 50 percent of the students said the best part of school was their teacher, Mrs. Bridges or Mrs. Fowler. Many of Lesley's and Carolyn's students also mentioned how much they loved learning to knit and play the piano with their teacher. The student surveys emphasize the importance that the teachers made in student learning.

Figure 5.14
End-of-Year
Student Survey

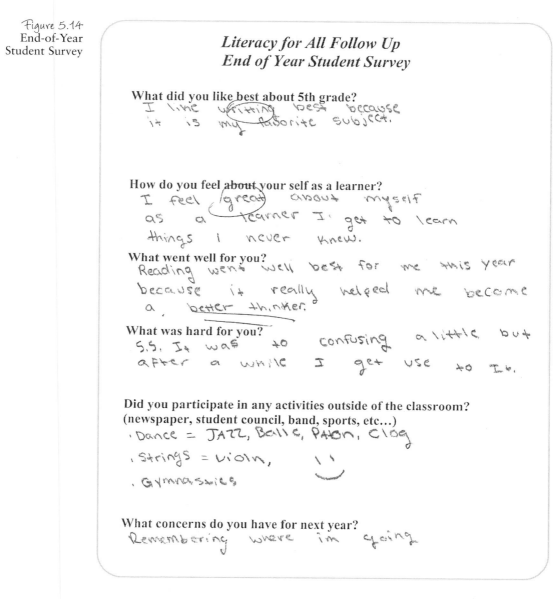

Literacy for All Follow Up
End of Year Student Survey

What did you like best about 5th grade?
I like writing best because it is my favorite subject.

How do you feel about your self as a learner?
I feel great about myself as a learner I get to learn things I never knew.

What went well for you?
Reading went well best for me this year because it really helped me become a better thinker.

What was hard for you?
S.S. It was to confusing a little but after a while I get use to It.

Did you participate in any activities outside of the classroom? (newspaper, student council, band, sports, etc…)
. Dance = JAZZ, Ballc, PABN, Clog
. Strings = viojn,
. Gymnassics

What concerns do you have for next year?
Remembering where im going

Literacy Intervention Room End-of-Year Student Survey
- What did you like best about fourth and fifth grade?
- How do you feel about yourself as a learner?
- What went well for you?
- What was hard for you?
- What concerns do you have for next year?

Defining Success

Four years later, the literacy classrooms are still in place. We were able to reduce the number of students needing additional literacy support and provide them with an instructional model designed to meet their learning needs. Local assessments show that students in the intervention classroom make an average of three-year gains in reading over a two-year period. There are still a few students who leave the intervention room reading below grade-level standards, but they are armed with a wealth of new strategies that they can apply as readers. We still consider the intervention classrooms a temporary structure as we continue to improve student achievement throughout the district. Our goal is eventually to remove the intervention rooms as we reduce the number of students needing additional support. In the meantime, this creative intervention works within the limited resources of our school and continues to meet the learning needs of the students, giving me the time and flexibility to support classroom instruction.

CHAPTER SIX

Coaching in Classrooms

The most important feature of an educator is to provide the
conditions under which people's learning curves go off the chart.
Sometimes it is the other people's learning curves: those of
students, teachers, parents, administrators. But at all times it is
our own learning curve.

ROLAND BARTH

I sat in the corner of the room in early December watching Lucy, a first-year teacher, present a lesson to her third-grade students. The class was quiet, but as I looked around, I quickly realized that every child had his or her own agenda. I watched Marvin sitting in the back of the room, hunched over with his desk on his back. Phillip was flicking his pencil with his finger. Bradley was ripping papers into tiny shreds and blowing them on the floor. Three other students had their hands raised to go to the bathroom. Darianne had her hands wrapped around her neck to indicate that she was dying of thirst. Paper littered the floor everywhere.

I was overwhelmed with the quiet chaos of the room. Lucy continued her writing lesson on crafting lead sentences to this third-grade class, even though she was the only one doing any work or thinking. At the end of forty-five minutes I slipped out of the room not knowing exactly what feedback I would share with Lucy later when we discussed what I saw. I wondered how to be constructive. I didn't want to crush her, since she had asked me to observe a lesson and was looking for my "expert" opinion.

Many times literacy specialist positions are created with the unspoken agenda of "fixing" teachers—new ones like Lucy who are overwhelmed, and veterans who are burned out. But I have never seen my role as that of fixer in supporting teachers. Instead, I strive to create conditions and conversations where teachers can get the support they need. I was able to help Lucy over time (more on her later in the chapter), but only after traveling a long road of letting teachers teach me how to support them.

Getting Started in Classrooms

When I changed from being a classroom teacher to literacy specialist, I remember looking at an empty schedule for my first week on the job. There were plenty of new students who needed to be screened, but it was an unnatural feeling not being locked into a schedule to work with students. I knew that part of my job was to work with teachers within the classroom setting, but I wasn't sure how to "get into" the classrooms.

One of the teachers with whom I had worked for ten years had just transferred from a multiage classroom to grade 5. Terry had twenty-five years of teaching experience but was nervous about working with this new grade level and within a new school. She was my first "in." I jumped on her invitation to start the school year in her room. Because we had just started *Strategies That Work* as the staff text, Terry wanted to experiment with the explicit teaching of comprehension strategies. We decided that I would go in weekly for the first six weeks and that together we would kick off an author study on Chris Van Allsburg and introduce reading comprehension strategies to her students. She didn't need me as a literacy expert in her room. She needed a colleague, sounding board, and friend to take the plunge with her in this new teaching assignment. Over the year, I continued to collaborate with her in the classroom as she designed her literacy program. I also found resources that would complement her teaching. Being invited into Terry's room gave me the quick sense of belonging that I needed, a place to try out new literacy and coaching strategies. It was from this early experience that I learned to go where I was wanted.

I found in the beginning that the teachers who invited me into their rooms were already "expert" teachers and confident in their own abilities in the classroom. These teachers welcomed the collaboration and conversations about instructional practices. I was grateful to be collaborating and learning with them and flattered that they wanted to work with me in their rooms. I knew that in time I would be able to get into other classrooms if and when the word got out among teachers that I was actually a beneficial resource.

Working in classrooms is all about building relationships and establishing trust over time. Lyons and Pinnell write, "Coaches need to maintain teachers' trust while having good communication with the supervisor" (Lyons and Pinnell 2001).

Eventually I began working in all types of classrooms for all different purposes. I always entered a classroom partnership with a teacher on an invitation basis, but that's not to say that I won't seek out opportunities to get into rooms. I might also approach teachers and ask if they can use me. The point is that I started slow, working in only a handful of classrooms my first year, and expanded to new and different classrooms over the next five years.

Coaching and Collaborating

I go into classrooms as a response to teacher needs. Timing is everything. When a teacher asks for help, I try to accommodate him or her as soon as possible. Because I am always busy, working in classrooms requires me to constantly reprioritize needs. If teachers who have never asked me into their rooms finally come forward with an invitation, I jump on the opportunity and rearrange my schedule to meet their needs immediately. Their desire or willingness to have me in their room would slip away if I told them I wasn't available for another two months.

When teachers ask if I can work in their room, my response is usually, "What is it that you want to explore together?" My philosophy toward supporting classroom instruction is the same approach I take with all learning—that the desire to learn and change needs to stem from an individual teacher. See Figure 6.1 for Neufeld and Roper's essential features of coaching strategies.

Rebecca, a third-grade teacher, was looking for an opportunity for collaboration and shared thinking. She knew that she could use me as a resource and that I would model new strategies in the classroom, even though she would set the course for her learning. Rebecca had read *Literature Circles* by Harvey Daniels and was interested in trying literature

Figure 6.1

ESSENTIAL FEATURES OF COACHING STRATEGIES

- They must be grounded in inquiry, reflection, and experimentation that are participant driven.
- They must be collaborative, involving a sharing of knowledge among educators and a focus on teachers' communities of practice rather than on individual teachers.
- They must be sustained, ongoing, intensive, and supported by modeling, coaching, and the collective solving of specific problems of practice.
- They must be connected to and derived from teachers' work with their students.
- They must engage teachers in concrete tasks of teaching, assessment, observation, and reflection that illuminate the process of learning and development.
- They must be connected to other aspects of school change.

In *Coaching: A Strategy for Developing Instructional Capacity* by Barbara Neufeld and Dana Roper, The Aspen Institute Program on Education (2003, p. 3)

discussion groups with her students and wanted my support in implementing them.

Meeting with Rebecca: Developing a Plan

Before working in Rebecca's classroom, we met and talked about implementing literature discussions groups. We looked at how we could adapt the concepts outlined in *Literature Circles* to meet the needs of her third-grade students. We decided to train her students by introducing the roles to the whole class, one role at a time, over the course of six weeks. We wanted to teach her students explicit comprehension strategies that would deepen their understanding for the stories they read and at the same time teach them strategies that would enhance their student-led literature discussions. We thought that introducing the roles of connector, questioner, passage master, and illustrator would work to accomplish this. Figure 6.2 shows the six-week plan Rebecca and I developed.

SIX-WEEK PLAN FOR IMPLEMENTING LITERATURE CIRCLES

We decided to use the book *Fables* by Arnold Lobel. This book is made up of many fables that are only a page long. The purpose was to teach the students the various literature roles. It was decided to use short text so that students could easily read the one page story and then practice the literature role that was being introduced. Each week the literature role would be introduced to the whole class.

Week 1 Introduce the role of "Connector"

- I introduced and modeled the role of *connector* using a short fable from *Fables* to the whole class.
- Students used the role sheet for *connector* to record their thinking while reading a short text. Role sheets were used the week the role was introduced. Students were transitioned to holding their thinking on Post-its.
- Students broke into small groups and talked about the connections they made to the text. I assigned a student facilitator just to keep the discussion going and to make sure everyone had an opportunity to participate.
- Students practiced the role of connector during the rest of the week with Rebecca using other short text.

Week 2 Introduce the role of "Questioner"

- I introduced and modeled the role of *questioner* using a short fable from *Fables*. I introduced students to questioning strategies and types of questions that deepen our understanding for a story (literal, inferential, and evaluative).
- Students used the role sheet for *questioner* to record their thinking while reading a short text.
- Students prepared for the role of connector by labeling their Post-it "connector" and writing down their thinking.
- Students broke into small groups and talked about the connections they made to the text and questions they had about the story.
- Students practiced the roles of connector and questioner during the rest of the week with the teacher using other short text.

Week 3 Introduce the role of "Passage Master"

- I introduced and modeled the role of *passage master* using a short fable from *Fables*.
- Students used the role sheet for *passage master* to record their thinking while reading a short text.
- Students prepared for the roles of connector and questioner by labeling separate Post-its "connector" and "questioner" and writing down their thinking.
- Students broke into small groups and talked about the connections, questions, and passages that stuck out to them in the story.

continued

Figure 6.2

- Students practiced the roles of connector, questioner, and passage master during the rest of the week with the teacher using other short text.

Week 4 Introduce the role of "Illustrator"

- I introduced and modeled the role of *illustrator* using a short fable from *Fables*.
- Students used the role sheet for *illustrator* to record their thinking while reading a short text. Students were asked to label their pictures using words from the text that they used to generate their pictures.
- Students prepared for the roles of connector, questioner, and passage master by labeling separate Post-its "connector," "questioner," and "passage master" and writing down their thinking.
- Students broke into small groups and talked about the connections, questions, passages, and illustrations they made as they read the text.
- Students practiced the roles of connector, questioner, passage master, and illustrator during the rest of the week with the teacher using other short text.

Week 5 Students prepare for literature discussions by practicing all four roles

- I came in and shared a short piece of text. I modeled how I prepared for all four literature roles and how I held my thinking on Post-its.
- Students practiced all four literature roles using a short piece of text. They were weaned off literature role sheets and held their thinking on Post-its. Students came prepared to discuss all four roles.
- Students practiced during the week with their teacher during literature groups.

Week 6 Students prepare for literature discussions by choosing a role of their choice

- During this week I came in during literature group time and followed the lead of the teacher. I circulated to talk with kids, making sure they understood the various literature group roles. I no longer led demonstrations.
- Students were weaned of role sheets and prepared for literature groups using Post-its to hold their thinking.
- Students now had the choice of coming to group preparing a role of their choice. The teacher still chose a student facilitator to help the flow of conversation. The hope was that students would choose to prepare for the role they most closely identified with during the reading and that allowing choice would foster a more natural literature discussion. All students were expected to come to group prepared. The idea was that when the conversation flowed to making connections, preparation for the connector role would allow them to add to the conversation using their notes to guide the discussion.

Figure 6.2
continued

Getting Started in the Classroom: Modeling for Rebecca and Her Students

I went into Rebecca's room once a week for six weeks, introducing and modeling literature group roles with her students. As the classroom teacher, Rebecca always stayed in the room and participated in the lesson. I always let the kids know we were trying out some new ideas. I wanted students to see this as a collaborative effort and that I was actually teaming with their teacher.

Follow-Up and Practice

Rebecca reinforced the lessons during the week when I was gone. We had incorporated additional practice of the literature roles with her students in our initial plan. The "practice" nudged Rebecca to try the roles with her students on her own, without being watched. It was a safe way for Rebecca to reinforce and practice the strategy before I came in the following week. The follow-up was an important element of the plan because research indicates that teachers need consistent practice in their own work settings (Fullan 1991).

Debriefing

Rebecca and I debriefed every week on our implementation of literature roles. This was an informal meeting, usually in her room at the end of the day. I always asked if the format was working for her. I encouraged her to personalize the implementation of literature discussions and make it her own. In the beginning she found that her students had trouble with taking notes for the roles on the three-by-three-inch Post-its, so we switched to a larger, three-by-five-inch size. The larger Post-its seemed to work well for the students, giving them more room to write. We also played around with colored Post-its, using different colors to represent different roles. Rebecca especially liked introducing the literature roles one at a time and to the whole group. She had tried introducing the four roles at once during literature groups and struggled with getting the discussions up and running. The continual debriefing between Rebecca and me prompted us to keep refining the delivery of instruction to the students and helped Rebecca make the implementation of literature discussions her own.

It's important that adequate modeling and guided practice occur if a lasting change in classroom instruction is going to take place. Teachers,

Figure 6.3

DEFINING HIGH-QUALITY PROFESSIONAL DEVELOPMENT

According to research by the U.S. Department of Education, high-quality professional development prepares teachers for the specific challenges when it

1. is of sufficient length, frequency, and intensity;
2. revolves around helping teachers move their students toward their state's content and performance standards;
3. gives teachers a central role in planning their own professional development; and
4. provides teachers with ample opportunity to practice skills and activities.

From *Improving the Odds: A Report on Title I from the Independent Review Panel* (2001, p. 9)

like students, need practice and repetition of new strategies to acquire fluency and automaticity to ensure that the changes in classroom practice will be lasting. Practice needs to be part of their professional development, according to research cited in Figure 6.3.

Research by Joyce and Showers shows that it took twenty to twenty-five trials in the classroom before new instructional practices became part of a teacher's routine (Dole 2004). By the end of my six weeks with Rebecca she was the one leading the lessons and organizing the student discussions, and I was the one lending the extra set of hands in the background. Figure 6.4 shows a framework for how specialists can support classroom teachers.

Figure 6.4

COLLABORATIVE FRAMEWORK FOR SUPPORTING TEACHERS IN THE CLASSROOM

- Meet with the teacher and design a plan for collaboration
- Model strategy for the teacher and students
- Practice of strategy by the teacher as follow-up
- Debrief with the classroom teacher
- Repetition of modeling and practice to acquire mastery

Time Frames

I find that going in once a week works well. This provides the teacher with an opportunity to try out the idea once or twice before I return the following week. Sometimes I go into a room for a six-week period to work on a writing project, or to try out a new reading strategy. Last year I went into Mary's fourth-grade classroom twice a week for six weeks. Mary and I taught the students strategies to hold their thinking using Post-its and highlighters. We also worked with students to find evidence in the text to support their thinking. These were strategies that surfaced during a study group on strategic reading using *I Read It, but I Don't Get It* by Cris Tovani. Even though Tovani works with older students, we knew we could use the same strategies with students in grades 4 and 5. Mary wanted to give these ideas a try, using me as support. Strategic reading was new territory, because Mary was comfortable using a more traditional model of having students answer questions and look up new vocabulary at the end of each chapter.

In classrooms with teachers who are looking to make structural and organizational changes to their literacy programs, my work in their room might span a three-year period. One third-grade teacher had recently transferred from fifth grade. Stacy was finding it difficult to adjust to the different curriculum and instructional demands for the younger children.

One day, she shared her frustration about the number of students reading and writing below grade level in her room. She thought she was not meeting their needs and that she was not adequately familiar with the resources in the school. I took this situation as an opportunity to offer her support. I told her that I couldn't offer her more tutoring time but that I could offer her "me," and that I could come in once a week for forty-five minutes to support her during literacy instruction. Stacy agreed, and we started talking about what she saw as her strengths and needs for her overall literacy program and started our work together.

Three years later I am still working in Stacy's classroom one day a week for forty-five minutes. I consider my work in her room a partnership. Sometimes I lead the whole class in a lesson, at times I work with small literature groups, and other times I watch as she starts the class with a mini-lesson for writer's workshop. Over the last two years she has redesigned her reading workshop and is now in the midst of working out the implementation of her writing workshop. Stacy will be the first one to admit that she struggles with organization and holding it together, but she continues to stretch herself as a teacher and explore new instructional strategies. As a result of talking through this teacher's needs, I was able to offer my support and establish a partnership with her.

Blanketing a Grade Level with a Strategy

Once in awhile my work in classrooms comes out of school in-service. An analysis of our fourth-grade state assessment data indicated that our students were unable to adequately respond to open-ended questions that required a well constructed answer. We decided to raise awareness of the issue with teachers in grades 3 through 5. During a school in-service, teachers were given released test questions. Teachers spent time looking at questions, becoming familiar with rubrics and anchor papers, and read released student papers.

In-Service Agenda
1. Teachers looked at released state questions for fourth-grade test
2. Staff scored released student papers using the state rubric
3. Staff identified the strengths and weaknesses of the papers

As a result of the in-service session, we decided to explore strategies that would better prepare our students to respond to constructed response questions. After looking through multiple resources, we decided to use the model developed by Ardith Cole in the book *Better Answers* as a strategy for answering questions that required a structured written response. The model is shown in Figure 6.5.

Before introducing the model to the staff, I experimented with the formula in Carolyn's fourth-grade literacy intervention room to see how it would work with students. The formula gave students an internal framework to answer questions and could be applied across content areas. By teaching Carolyn's fourth graders, I was able to break down the formula and figure out the best way to introduce it to students.

After introducing the Better Answer Formula to Carolyn's students I went back and shared it with teachers in another in-service. The purpose for taking this concept across schools and grade levels was to provide students an internal framework so that they could better access and communicate their thinking. We thought this was a beneficial strategy that could be used across content areas and not just for taking state assessments. Although we saw the value of a common constructed response format, we were cautious about investing too much time teaching students a "for-

Figure 6.5

BETTER ANSWER FORMULA, DEVELOPED BY ARDITH COLE

- **Restate the Question**

Students are taught to physically manipulate the question and identify what the question is asking.

- **Construct a Gist**

Students complete their restatement by constructing a general answer to the question that they will then support through their written constructed response. The restatement and the construction of the gist make up the topic sentence of the response.

- **Use Details to Support Your Answer**

Students use details/evidence to support their restatement.

- **Stay on Topic**

Students are expected to stay on topic and write to the question they are presented.

- **Use Proper Conventions**

Students are expected to use proper conventions even though the formula emphasizes message and a strategy for constructing a structured response to an open-ended question.

mula." We didn't want to overemphasize constructed response questions, but thought we had a responsibility to familiarize students with these types of questions and provide them with a strategy to answer them. It was a result of this in-service that third-grade teachers asked if I could introduce the Better Answer Formula to all seven grade 3 classrooms.

In-Service Agenda
1. Introduced the Better Answer Formula model to teachers
2. Teachers practiced the Better Answer Formula model
3. Teachers applied the Better Answer Formula to released state test questions

After providing the in-service to the teachers on the Better Answer Formula, I started working with each third-grade classroom. I went into each classroom once a week for six weeks. I introduced students to the Better Answer Formula, teaching them how to read through questions and identify what the prompts were asking of them. Students then practiced the formula. We also looked at how they could apply this model to any assignment. After working in each classroom, I provided teachers with the materials that I used with their students so that they could teach the format themselves the following year. Figure 6.6 outlines the framework for teaching the constructed response model.

By taking this approach and blanketing a grade level, we were able to provide timely instruction to the one hundred fifty students in grade 3. We knew at the end of the year that all the grade 3 students had tried out this strategy and would have had some familiarity with it before being required to take the state assessments in fourth grade. After providing school-based in-service and classroom support, teachers felt comfortable incorporating the Better Answer Formula within their own instruction to students the following year.

Collaborating with Master Teachers

One of the bonuses of my position is that I get to work with so many highly skilled veteran teachers. I have found that these teachers crave professional conversations and collaboration. Because teachers typically spend their days working alone with students, there is never time to process new ideas and thinking. What these teachers want is someone to talk with and challenge their thinking.

Cathy, a fifth-grade teacher who was introduced in Chapter 3, just wanted the opportunity for ongoing conversations. In addition to our chats before and after school, I told her I would like to come in once a week during writing workshop. She was thrilled that I would actually take time out of my schedule for her classroom. I was flattered that she thought I had something to offer. The initial purpose of my presence was nothing more than to be an extra set of eyes and ears for writing conferences.

Our yearlong partnership turned into ongoing conversations about ways to document writing growth through student portfolios and identifying strengths and needs of her students as writers. In time I started to teach occasional mini-lessons so she could be freed up to sit back and watch her own students during the lesson. We often talked across the room, modeling our own thinking aloud for students. The students saw collaboration. Cathy and I felt comfortable enough to interject and add to each other's

Figure 6.6

TEACHING THE CONSTRUCTED RESPONSE MODEL

Adapted from Better Answer Formula by Ardith Cole in *Better Answers*

Better Answer Formula

- Restate the question.
- Construct a gist answer.
- Use details to support your answer.
- Stay on topic and write a constructed response.
- Use proper conventions.

This strategy takes about six weeks to introduce to students. We start by having students work with personal questions and gradually move them to working with short text that requires them to extract evidence from the text to support their thinking.

Week 1	**Introduce Restating the Question**
	• Students practice restating the question.
	What is your favorite thing to do in the winter?
	My favorite thing to do in winter is . . .
Week 2	**Introduce Constructing a Gist Answer**
	• Students practice restating the question.
	• Students practice constructing a gist answer.
	My favorite thing to do in winter is play outside with my kids.
Week 3	**Introduce How to Use Details to Support Your Answer**
	• Students practice restating the question.
	• Students practice constructing a gist answer.
	• Students generate supporting details for their response.
	My favorite thing to do in winter is play outside with my kids.
	• Walking in the snow after a storm
	• Making snow angels
	• Walking in the woods
Week 4	**Introduce Putting the Formula Together to Stay on Topic and Write a Constructed Response**
	Students use their work generated over the last three weeks to write a constructed response on their favorite thing to do in the winter.
Weeks 5, 6	**Students Write Constructed Responses to Questions Using Short Text**
	Fables by Arnold Lobel used as source for short texts

ideas and thinking during lessons. She often caught me in the hall to share her thinking on how she was contemplating making a change in her literacy program. I don't think she was looking for any answers from me. There was no expectation that I was an expert or that I was supposed to be coaching her to make any changes. She was teaching me, and we were generating new ideas together. By being available to her, I offered her time to reflect on her own classroom. It was a valuable experience for me, because she is truly a gifted writing teacher.

Cathy and I have also had our disagreements. Last year Cathy struggled with how we administer our local writing prompts. She disagreed philosophically about the time restraints and using on-demand writing as part of our evaluation system of local data on writing. She didn't think it was a fair assessment. We could have stopped there, frustrated with each other, feeling that the other didn't understand our point of view. Instead we continued talking about the writing prompts and the fact that if you administer an assessment only once a year, students have not had adequate opportunity to be familiar with the task. I shared the research from Ellin Keene. Keene says students should be writing on demand about 30 percent of the time (Morgan with Odom 2004). We ended the year with the plan that we would work together the following year and incorporate on-demand writing throughout the year in her classroom, demystifying this process for students.

Cathy then brought her concerns about writing prompts and our ideas to the fifth-grade teachers. As a team they listened, and they too decided to work on incorporating on-demand writing throughout the year. Too often as educators we remain quiet and shut our doors when we disagree with one another. Yet when we establish trust within relationships, it is much easier to agree to work through professional disagreements and find common ground.

Supporting New Teachers

The needs of new teachers entering the district are different from those of established teachers within the school. In addition to supporting new teachers on best literacy practices, I also have to "catch them up" on district and school initiatives. As new teachers come on board I need to help them become familiar with district goals, school procedures, curriculum, and the local assessments they will be expected to administer. A new teacher has to take in a lot of information when entering a new school district, because every district and school has their own way of doing things.

Even before school starts, new teachers are whisked from in-service to in-service, bombarded with procedural expectations. I need to support new teachers in literacy, but I also want to give them time to build their own classroom communities and establish relationships with their students. New teachers are also assigned mentor teachers, so I don't want to overwhelm them with too much support.

My initial strategy in supporting new teachers is to work behind the scenes and out of their classrooms. I spend time reviewing fall literacy assessments and provide training and support as teachers administer the assessments so they can set instructional goals for their students.

New teachers are also invited to participate in study groups that start meeting in October. The study group offers an informal opportunity to ask questions and share their thinking with more seasoned teachers on staff. Their questions often inspire experienced teachers to reexamine their instructional practices. New teachers start to build collegiality with their peers as a result of their participation in a group.

Once new teachers get through fall assessments, they need to prepare for parent/teacher conferences. During this time I often work with new teachers as they develop student portfolios, which they use as evidence of student achievement during the conferences.

By December new teachers have had a chance to establish their classroom environment, feel more comfortable within the school, and made it through their first parent conferences. I start to ask new teachers if I can lend them an extra hand in their classrooms.

Most new teachers are receptive to the invitation and take me up on the offer. By December they are able to identify areas that they want to work on with me. They want help as they wrestle with fitting everything into a school day. They wrestle with their schedules and setting up their literacy blocks.

I usually start by just going into the classrooms once a week. I want to follow their lead and get a sense of their teaching style before we start tweaking their reading and writing workshop blocks. I am usually amazed at their openness to feedback and their enthusiasm to take on new challenges.

After I've gone into a room for a few weeks, the teacher usually zeros in on a specific area that he or she wants to explore. We start small. Together the teacher and I decide how I will continue lending support in their classroom. Often new teachers welcome the opportunity to sit back and watch me model leading a literature group discussion or writing lesson.

I often work with new teachers for the rest of the year on a weekly basis. My work won't end with them at the end of the year. I find that new teachers are usually excited to start fresh the next year. We start planning in the spring how we can start the next school year together. New teachers need opportunities for repetition and support so they can maintain a cohesive literacy framework independently without my support. I try to support new teachers for at least two years as they become more confident literacy teachers. See Figure 6.7 for some tips on working in individual classrooms.

Revisiting Lucy's Classroom

Let's get back to Lucy, the first-year teacher with classroom management problems I introduced at the start of this chapter. Lucy was excited, idealistic, and passionate about incorporating best literacy practice into her classroom. Although she wanted feedback and begged for my honest opinion of her room, I found myself speechless and tiptoeing around the issue of management the first few times I went into her classroom. Instead, I complimented her on her willingness to dive into writer's workshop, and praised her for the models of writing that she shared with the children. I encouraged her to break her lessons into smaller chunks and to get students actively involved so that they were not spending long periods of time listening. I could see her trying to implement my suggestions every time I went back into her room. But the negative behaviors were also escalating, and management issues were interfering with student learning.

One day Lucy brought up the subject of the student behaviors in her class and asked me for any suggestions on tackling the problem. She shared that the principal had told her that if she didn't pull it together, she wouldn't be offered a contract the following year. I felt awful for Lucy, because I knew it was true. At the same time part of me wondered if she could really pull the class back on track this far into the school year. It was going to take a lot of work to get the students to respond to a behavior management plan while laying out the organizational structures for literacy in her room. But Lucy had the desire and drive to make it work. I thought I would fail if I did not give it my all. I needed to commit myself to helping Lucy regain control of her classroom, and help her establish the writer's workshop at the same time.

Lucy and I decided that I would start leading her writer's workshop. Lucy was part of the study group that was exploring *The Revision Toolbox* by Georgia Heard. She had heard about the "My Life in Seven Stories"

Figure 6.7

TIPS FOR GOING INTO CLASSROOMS

- **Go Where You Are Invited**

I always start with teachers who want the support and invite me to work in their classrooms.

- **Be on Time**

Working in classrooms is a priority. I am always on time for my classroom work. I never want to leave a teacher and twenty students waiting for me!

- **Follow Through**

If I say I am going to prepare materials or follow up with additional resources, then I do so in a timely manner. I always follow through for teachers.

- **Don't Make a Teacher Wait if They Are Asking for Help**

If a teacher asks for help, I will often rearrange my schedule to accommodate them.

- **Always Ask the Teacher if the Plan Is Working for Them**

I never assume that my style works for all classrooms. If a teacher is going to adopt a new literacy practice, it needs to work for his or her teaching style and may need to be tweaked.

- **Take Time to Talk**

It's important to make the time to debrief on what is happening in the classroom. It may be a short informal chat, but it is important to process the collaboration in the classroom.

- **Build Trust**

Trust takes time. I think trust is established if I do what I say I am going to do. It goes back to being on time, following through, and supporting teachers when they ask for help.

project that I had developed the previous year. We decided this would be an appropriate starting point for the writer's workshop because we needed a little more structure. We simply wanted to get these kids working and writing. We also hoped to hook her students on writing through their own personal stories. The side benefits of this project would be to increase their volume of writing and introduce them to various revision strategies. I began working in Lucy's room twice a week. The plan was for me to lead the days that I was in the room and for her to lead and follow through on the writing on the days that I was not there.

I was scared to lead demonstration lessons in Lucy's room. I was afraid I had lost all of my tricks of classroom management. The first day I led the writing workshop in her room, I walked in and set my ground rules. There would be no drinks or bathroom breaks when I was in the room. I also told them not to raise their hands. Lucy and I would be around and see all of them. I did this because I had observed that students spent most of their time with their hands up. Lucy would run from student to student, helping them think of what to write about. I brought new writer's notebooks for each student and praised them for just writing their names on their drafts. Tasks were broken into tiny pieces.

As I began the lesson on generating ideas for stories, Darianne immediately asked for a drink of water, testing my rule of no drinks. Darianne pleaded with Lucy for a drink. Lucy glanced at me and I shook my head. Darianne turned purple as she pressed her fingers into the side of her throat. Lucy glanced at me again, making sure that I saw the situation. I shook my head again. I thought to myself, Great, this girl is going to pass out or throw up. I kept working and forgot about Darianne. I was too preoccupied with Bradley ripping up the new writer's notebook I had just given him. I ignored his behavior because I now saw John with his hand up. I ignored the hand, because he was one of the first students I'd had a conference with, and my rule was no hands raised for help.

I let John keep his hand raised for thirty minutes. Lucy then came up to me and whispered, "I just want you to know that his mother is the parent volunteer in the room right now." I thought, Great—my luck. I let him keep his hand up because we had laid our ground rules. I had already met with him, and I could see that all he wanted to tell me was that I had left a piece of white paper on his desk.

Then there was Sophie, who declared that she didn't like to write. Somehow Sophie was excused to the nurse's room for feeling ill. She quickly returned and told me she was going home and reminded me that she didn't like to write. I wondered if anything I was doing was working, because they were testing every rule I had put in place. But then I saw Bradley. He had stopped ripping his paper and had picked up his pencil. I went right over to him and made a big deal over his idea about his friend's snake that had escaped from its cage. He wrote his title on the paper. He actually had a smile on his face, and you could tell he liked the praise. I couldn't believe he had actually started writing. Then I looked over at Darianne. I had forgotten all about her. She had been choking herself earlier in the period, yet now she was writing away. When I asked the students to stop writing, she raised her paper to show me that she had filled her whole paper with a story of a pet cat. I knew at that moment that this was going to work and that together Lucy and I could get these kids on track and producing work.

Over the next eight weeks, Lucy and I continued to implement "My Life in Seven Stories." We remained consistent in enforcing our ground rules. Soon students were writing for larger chunks of uninterrupted time. They worked without asking to go to the bathroom. I was amazed at how quickly they adjusted to the procedures that we set in place. They were eager writers and proud to share their stories.

Lucy and I continued to work as a team on the writing project. We debriefed weekly on what was happening in her room and how each student was progressing. We even laughed with other teachers about some of the student behavior stories that we had tackled when our study group on strategic reading strategies met.

Lucy also made physical changes to her room based on our conversations, rearranging it to create a better learning space. She placed student desks in groups so that they could collaborate and talk about their writing. She had a dry-erase board mounted so that she could easily provide visual models for the kids. She continued to set up and personalize procedures and organizational structures within the writer's workshop that worked for her teaching style and students. As we worked together throughout the spring, we began to plan on how we would start up writer's workshop together in the fall. Working together on "My Life in Seven Stories" was only the beginning of our collaboration. I am happy to report that Lucy's contract was renewed.

Other Kinds of Support

Support doesn't always come in the form of working in a teacher's classroom. Sometimes supporting classroom instruction comes in the format of offering my time behind the scenes of the classroom. I work to make myself available to teachers before and after school. I am at school at least an hour before students. Often teachers drop by in the morning or after school to talk through their thinking of a new idea, or because they need help finding resources to support a lesson.

I've helped teachers redesign the layout of their classrooms, and reorganized classroom libraries. Other times I go book buying for teachers, or help a teacher short on time with a purchase order. Recently a new teacher even asked me to meet her at the bookstore over Labor Day weekend so that we could buy books together. When she shared the story with her husband, he thought I was crazy to join her on a holiday weekend. I never thought twice about the fact that it was the weekend—it was her weekend, too! Other times teachers are looking to strengthen a section of their classroom libraries and ask me to find books in a particular genre. I look for professional development opportunities for teachers outside of school, and will even attend conferences with teachers if they want someone to go with them. I sometimes laminate materials or bind student books for teachers, if the finishing details are the extra steps it takes to help them complete a project.

Supporting Change

My rewards come from the teachers and students who become excited about their learning. Recently Lucy came up to me and said, "Thank you. For the first time in my teaching career I feel good about what I am doing. I was also offered a teaching contract for another year." She then handed me a crumpled little piece of paper from one of her students. As I walked down the hall, I read the note. It said, "Mrs. Allen is great. She taught me how to do snapshots and revision strategies. Thank you very very much, Mrs. Allen. From Nick." It just doesn't get any better than that for me.

CHAPTER SEVEN

The Fluency Awareness Project: Piloting Reform Initiatives

*Ms. Washington would read to us every day after lunch, and her
voice was like ten different musical instruments. She could make
her voice go low and deep and strong like a tuba, or hop, hop,
hop quick and light like a flute.*

*When she'd read, her voice wrapped around my head and my
heart, and it softened and lightened everything up. It put a pain
in my heart that felt good. When she told stories it made me
want to tell stories. I wanted to read like her, so that I could have
that feeling anytime.*

EXCERPT FROM IDA B, KATHERINE HANNIGAN

Josh read to me from *Lost on a Mountain in Maine* by Donn Fendler.
His reading was labored and slow. I found it painful to listen to this
fourth-grade student as he struggled to work through the text. At the
end of the page he looked up at me and said, "I did good. I got all the
words right!"

Josh had actually read the passage with 100 percent word accuracy,
but upon probing I was not surprised to uncover that he had little under-

standing for what he had read. All of his energy had gone into reading the words on the page. Unfortunately, Josh was not an isolated case. I found myself assessing more and more students who struggled with reading fluency in the intermediate grades.

Many of these students appeared to have adequate decoding skills, but their laborious reading rate, poor phrasing, and lack of expression were affecting their ability to work through extended text. These students lacked reading stamina!

This observation was confirmed when analyzing student results of the newly adopted reading assessment in our district, the Developmental Reading Assessment (DRA). The DRA assesses the four components of fluency: expression, phrasing, rate, and accuracy. I found that we had a population of struggling readers that scored a 99 percent accuracy rate but fell in the slow range for reading rate (less than 90 wpm). Students also read with little expression and poor phrasing.

When talking with classroom teachers about the students I was seeing with slow reading rates, they shared that these kids also struggled to complete assignments in class. These students worked slowly, often becoming disengaged from texts and assignments. Their poor reading fluency was affecting their overall school performance.

Here is the problem as articulated by Kylene Beers in her book, *When Kids Can't Read, What Teachers Can Do.* A typical silent reading rate for a sixth-grade student is 160–190 words per minute.

> *You read at a rate of 60 words per minute. You have 10 pages of homework to read. Each page of homework has 500 words (social studies textbook, science textbook, and literature book). How long will it take you to complete your homework? Got it? You'll spend 83 minutes, or 1 hour and 23 minutes just reading 10 pages. And that's presuming that it's 10 pages that are at your independent level. (Beers 2002, pp. 209–210)*

That is almost an hour and a half just to read your homework, not complete the assignment! Although oral reading rates are generally slower than silent reading rates, they offer insight into the phrasing, expression, and intonation students use as they read (Beers 2002).

Kylene Beers's example of the effect of poor reading rates scared me. I knew that the population of students that Beers described would soon be our fourth- and fifth-grade students, some to move into middle school. These students would be faced with an increased volume of reading and textbook demands and be at risk for school failure if we didn't start to address this issue of reading fluency.

Over the previous few years we had given a great deal of attention at the intermediate level to reading comprehension strategies. Yet we had provided these same students with virtually no strategies to strengthen reading stamina as they transitioned to longer and more extended texts. Compounding the issue was teachers' reduction of independent reading time, because they no longer knew where to fit it into their packed school day. We wrongly assumed that because students could read the words on a page and demonstrated an understanding of what they had read on a short reading passage, they could maintain this performance over longer and more complete texts. At the same time, we wondered why it took some students forever to finish classroom assignments or why students attempted assignments without actually ever reading the assigned text. I knew that increasing fluency skills would be crucial to ensuring school success as these students made the leap to increased textbook reading in sixth grade.

Using Technology to Support Fluency Instruction

Peter Redmond, a technology consultant for our school, came up with the idea to explore reading fluency through the use of innovative technology. Peter was a retired fourth-grade teacher with more than thirty years of classroom experience who held advanced degrees in special education and technology with a specialty in literacy instruction. Peter was especially interested in the research put forth by the National Reading Panel that indicated that fluency instruction was one of the five essential components of an effective reading program (National Institute of Child Health and Human Development 2000).

Peter approached me to collaborate and I was quick to jump on board. As technology consultant, Peter would focus on the technical side of visually documenting the oral reading fluency of students through the use of technology. As literacy specialist, I would support the project by creating an instructional framework for teaching oral reading fluency to students and teachers at the intermediate grades. The project would integrate literacy and technology as a vehicle to help drive instruction.

Peter and I familiarized ourselves with the newest research in fluency. The research validated our suspicions of the negative effect poor reading fluency may be having on our struggling readers at the intermediate grades.

Richard Allington (2001) notes that struggling readers often lack fluency, and even though the skill can be taught, it is often neglected during reading instruction (Strickland, Ganske, and Monroe 2002). We wanted students to understand what it meant to be a fluent reader, but the ultimate focus of this project was the teachers. Our goal was to gently nudge them toward incorporating deliberate reading fluency instruction within their classrooms.

Project Outline

Three classrooms were invited to participate in the fluency awareness project: one regular fourth-grade classroom and both literacy intervention classrooms (fourth and fifth grades).

Videotaping Students

Students were videotaped in the fall and in the spring for comparative purposes. The first taping of students was done in October before any instruction on oral reading fluency. Participating teachers were asked to select an appropriate text in which students could read the selected text with at least 95 percent accuracy (Rasinski 2003). Peter videotaped each student individually reading an excerpt (150 words) of text from this teacher-selected literature. The oral reading rate was calculated at the time of taping for each student.

Whole-Class Lesson: What Is Fluency?

Timothy Rasinski defines fluency as "the ability to read accurately, quickly, effortlessly, and with appropriate expression and meaning" (2003). Peter and I went into each of the classrooms and presented a whole-group lesson on the components of fluency (expression, phrasing, rate, and accuracy). We talked with students about reading fluency and worked to define what these components meant in terms of their oral and silent reading behaviors. Students were able to articulate that their teachers were fluent readers. Students cited that daily read-aloud by their teacher was an excellent model for oral reading fluency.

Students were introduced to the Oral Reading Fluency Scale. This fluency scale was created specifically to be used with our students in fourth and fifth grades and was adapted from several oral reading fluency resources. See Figure 7.1. We discussed the language on the rubric and

ORAL READING FLUENCY SCALE

A fluent reader consistently reads accurately, quickly, effortlessly, and with appropriate expression and meaning. The reader maintains their performance over long periods of engaged reading (Rasinski 2003).

Name _____ Date _____

Oral Reading Fluency	Does Not Meet 1	Partially Meets 2	Meets 3	Exceeds 4
Expression	1 Little expression; monotone; Inappropriate hesitations and pauses	2 Some expression that conveys meaning; Breaks in smoothness	3 Expression that reflects mood, pace, and tension at times; Voice	4 Expression consistently reflects mood, pace, and tension
Phrasing	1 Short phrases *Word by word Improper stress and intonation*	2 Longer word phrases some of the time *Little choppy Pauses for breaths Rough spots*	3 Longer, meaningful phrases most of the time	4 Consistency longer, meaningful phrases
Rate (Pace) *WPM = Words Per Minute	1 Slow with long pauses and repetitions Less than 90 wpm (Grades 4 and 5)	2 Moderate rate with some pauses and repetitions OR inappropriately fast; Uneven pace 90–109 wpm (Grade 4) 90–114 wpm (Grade 5)	3 Adequate with a few pauses and/or repetitions 110–130 wpm (Grade 4) 115–135 wpm (Grade 5)	4 Very good Consistently appropriate Greater than 130 wpm (Grade 4) Greater than 135 wpm (Grade 5)
Accuracy Rate (150-Word Passage)	1 90–94% (9–12 Errors) Reader struggles with decoding words	2 95–96% (5–8 Errors)	3 97–98% (3–4 Errors)	4 99–100% (0–2 Errors) Reader decodes correctly and effortlessly

Fluency Scale created for grades 4 and 5. Rubric is adapted by J. Allen from Multidimensional Fluency Scale (T. Rasinski), Reading Rates by Barr (cited by K. Beers), and Oral Reading Fluency Rubric (DRA Teacher Observation Form).

Goal _____

_____

_____

Figure 7.1

broke it down so that students understood how their oral reading was being assessed. The classroom teacher also participated in this discussion. We wanted students to be aware of how they were being assessed for reading fluency.

Small-Group Viewing: Self-Assessment and Goal Session

The student video clips were exported onto a class VHS tape for easy viewing. Peter and I then facilitated student viewing and self-assessment sessions.

Students were pulled in small groups of three or four into the literacy room to watch their oral reading video clip. During this time we reviewed the components of oral reading fluency. We also generated a list of sample goals that could improve reading fluency. The small-group viewing process included watching the student video clips, identifying strengths of the readers, and the students' completion of the Oral Reading Fluency Scale (self-assessment).

Students were initially nervous about watching themselves on tape. They felt more comfortable once they trusted that the viewing session would truly highlight their strengths. Students used the Oral Reading Fluency Scale to self-assess themselves for expression and phrasing.

Kristen was the first student on the tape in the first group I facilitated in a fourth-grade classroom. She was a strong reader. At the end of her video clip, I asked the group to identify a strength Kristen demonstrated as a reader. One student shared that Kristen read with voice. You could see a smile immediately creep across Kristen's face. Starting with strengths established a safe environment for students to honestly reflect on themselves as readers. Kristen verbally stumbled a couple of times during her video clip. In her self-assessment she rated herself a 2 on the Oral Reading Fluency Scale and said that maybe if she practiced the passage, she could work out the phrasing.

The next student in the group, John, was weaker. The text seemed a bit difficult for him, and he read slowly in a monotone. As soon as his clip finished, John blurted out, "That was awful. I messed up and was too slow." Another student in the group immediately chimed in, "But John, you self-corrected your mistakes—that's a good thing." John seemed to perk up a little with the compliment. He identified that he needed to work on reading faster. Peter did a running record on each student as we watched the video clips and calculated the accuracy rate for each one. Students transferred the accuracy rate onto their rubric. Students were also given their reading rates, which were calculated during the taping session.

As students discussed the oral reading clip for each person in their group, they were supportive of one another and always remarked on the strengths that they noticed in their peers' reading. Once the students completed the fluency rubric, they set fluency goals for themselves. Examples of student goals included the following:

- My goal is to put more expression in my reading.
- Read a little louder and with more voice.
- My goal is to work on my reading so it is not so choppy.
- I need to read a little faster.
- I need to work on my breathing. It sounds funny.
- My goal is to read a little slower and with more expression.
- My goal is to have more expression and stop stuttering.

Storing and Accessing Student Video Clips

Student video clips were downloaded onto Apple iMovie software. Students were taught how to add titles and dates to their video clips. Students exported the iMovie as a Quick Time movie and added it to their digital portfolio, which was then shared with parents during parent/teacher conferences. A DVD was created for each teacher that displayed the fall and spring oral reading video clip of each student. This enabled students and the classroom teacher to view the fall and spring oral reading performances side by side, and to compare student growth from fall to spring.

Sharing Instructional Strategies

Strategies were shared with both teachers and students on how to improve oral reading fluency (strategies included rereading, read-aloud, reading books at independent level, reader's theater, poetry, and increased volume of reading engagement). I created an instructional resource binder to provide background knowledge on the topic of fluency and to guide teachers in incorporating fluency instruction into their classroom.

I not only wanted to provide teachers with ideas to improve reading fluency but also wanted teachers to understand how the lack of reading fluency affected students' school performance beyond third grade. The binder was broken into several sections: research articles to build background knowledge, tools to measure fluency, resources for analyzing running records, and instructional strategies to improve reading fluency.

RESOURCES THAT SUPPORT READING FLUENCY WORK

- Hudson, R., H. Lane, and P. Pullen. 2005. "Reading fluency assessment and instruction: What why and how?" *The Reading Teacher* 58, 702–714.
  This article provides the theoretical background for reading fluency and why it is an essential component to a literacy program.

- Griffith, L., and T. V. Rasinski. 2004. "A focus on fluency: How one teacher incorporated fluency with her reading curriculum." *The Reading Teacher* 58, 126–137.
  This article addresses the practical application of how one fourth-grade teacher incorporated fluency instruction into her classroom.

- Beers, K. 2002. *When Kids Can't Read, What Teachers Can Do: A Guide for Teachers 6–12.* Portsmouth, NH: Heinemann.
  In this book Beers addresses the importance of reading fluency for students in grades 6–12. The book provides resources for calculating oral and silent reading rates and strategies to improve reading fluency with older readers.

- Opitz, M., and T. V. Rasinski. 1998. *Good-Bye Round Robin: 25 Effective Oral Reading Strategies.* Portsmouth, NH: Heinemann.
  This book provides many practical ideas beyond the traditional round-robin oral reading format for incorporating oral reading fluency strategies in the classroom.

- Rasinski, T. V. 2003. *The Fluent Reader: Oral Reading Strategies for Building Word Recognition, Fluency, Comprehension.* New York: Scholastic.
  This is a comprehensive resource on reading fluency by Timothy Rasinski. It provides both the theoretical background for fluency and offers readers practical ideas for incorporating fluency instruction in the classroom. It contains several resources for measuring reading fluency including the Multidimensional Fluency Scale.

- Strickland, D., K. Ganske, and J. Monroe. 2002. *Supporting Struggling Readers and Writers: Strategies for Classroom Intervention 3–6.* Portland, ME: Stenhouse.
  This book provides many practical ideas for how to improve reading fluency for the struggling reader.

Figure 7.2

Incorporating Fluency into the Classroom

The teachers who participated in this project began emphasizing fluency instruction during different aspects of their day. Although each teacher already embedded literacy practices within their day that fostered fluency, they now made a more conscious commitment to the teaching of reading fluency and communicating its importance to their students. Each teacher zeroed in and focused on a different approach for improving fluency.

Improving Fluency Through Modeling Read-Aloud

Fourth-grade teacher Jill has always been passionate about read-aloud. She used her read-aloud as a vehicle to improve reading fluency (Strickland, Ganske, and Monroe 2002). Jill maximized her read-aloud time by reinforcing the components of reading fluency (expression, phrasing, rate, and word accuracy). It was through read-aloud that she modeled how adequate reading fluency enhances the meaning of the text. One technique Jill used for modeling expression was the use of various voices for different characters. By doing this she brought the characters alive for her students.

In reading the book *George's Marvelous Medicine* by Roald Dahl, Jill discussed with her students how the tone and mood of George's grandmother could be inferred through a reader's use of expression while reading the book. Through Jill's modeling it was clear that George's grandmother was not warm and nurturing toward George.

> *"It's not what you like or what you don't like," Grandma snapped. "It's what's good for you that counts. From now on, you must eat cabbage three times a day. Mountains of cabbage! And if it's got caterpillars in it, so much the better!" (p. 5)*

It was through Jill's modeling and facilitation of class discussions that students learned to infer the tone and mood of the story, gaining a greater appreciation for the characters.

To communicate the importance of fluency, Jill also modeled inappropriate fluency by making her reading slow and choppy, using a flat monotone. Her students immediately interrupted her reading and asked her what she was doing! Jill followed up by asking them how they felt as listeners when she read like that. Students shared that they couldn't keep track of the characters and didn't know what was going on in the story. One student replied, "Reading like that makes for chaos and confusion!"

Jill also seized opportunities to share with students the importance of reading stamina. On occasion she had student readers take over read-aloud for the class. On one particular day, when the student had finished, he announced to Jill in front of the class, "Reading like you is hard work and it's tiring! How do you do it for so long?" As a result of this comment Jill talked with the class about the importance of sustaining their reading over longer texts and confirmed that reading was hard work. Jill stressed that if readers simply read the words of the story without focusing on expression, phrasing, and rate, they will probably lose the meaning of the text and end up as the student had shared earlier—in chaos and confused.

Using Series Books to Improve Reading Stamina

Carolyn, the fourth-grade literacy intervention classroom teacher, used series books to improve reading fluency with her students. Carolyn's strategy to improve reading rate and stamina was to increase the amount of time that students were actively engaged reading high interest texts that were appropriately matched to their reading ability. Carolyn increased silent reading time from four days to five days a week (thirty minutes) and also built in a weekly homework assignment where students were asked to read aloud to their parents for twenty minutes.

The key to Carolyn's fluency instruction was finding accessible books that students were excited about reading. She worked hard to find books that would appeal to her students. Carolyn found that series books provided a great hook to get her reluctant readers engaged and reading (Szymusiak and Sibberson 2001). Once students got through the first book of the series, they usually begged for another book from the same series. See Figure 7.3 for series book suggestions.

One reason using series books was a successful technique for improving fluency was that students became familiar with the main characters and text structure, making the comprehension of the book much easier. Students didn't have to work so hard to understand what was happening

Figure 7.3

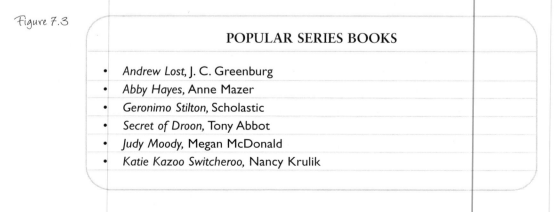

POPULAR SERIES BOOKS

- *Andrew Lost,* J. C. Greenburg
- *Abby Hayes,* Anne Mazer
- *Geronimo Stilton,* Scholastic
- *Secret of Droon,* Tony Abbot
- *Judy Moody,* Megan McDonald
- *Katie Kazoo Switcheroo,* Nancy Krulik

in the story, and they could put more energy into sustaining their reading and improving their overall fluency performance. Having students hook into a series was a great vehicle for having students improve their reading rates and ultimately their stamina for reading longer books.

Layering Texts to Improve Fluency in Content Areas

Lesley, the fifth-grade literacy intervention classroom teacher, focused on improving her students' fluency for reading informational texts. Lesley wanted to break down the barriers of content-area reading for her students. She knew that as her students moved on to sixth grade, they would be faced with the challenge of sustaining their reading in the content areas while tackling unfamiliar concepts and new vocabulary.

Lesley used the strategy of layering texts to build familiarity with concepts and vocabulary (Stead 2001). She introduced this strategy to the whole class through the topic of moving west (a fifth-grade curriculum requirement). She explicitly taught students the strategy of starting with "easy" reading material on the topic before having her students read the chapter from the textbook. Lesley provided students reading material at their independent reading level to support them as they built background knowledge. As students created a foundation for moving west, Lesley layered on harder texts until she thought they were ready for the textbook.

Lesley then had the students practice this strategy independently with individual research projects. She encouraged students to sort through their resources and start with materials that were the easiest to read and understand. I recall one of her students, Dakota, giving an informal class briefing on his topic of Mount Everest. He talked to his class about the dangers of Everest and how hikers needed to be cautious of the Khumba Icefall and crevasses. He shared the story of Tenzing Norgay and Edmond Hillary and the porters and sherpas used to support their trip to the summit. I listened in amazement as this new vocabulary flowed from his mouth. I was equally impressed with his fluency as he read excerpts from *Life* magazine. Just think—Dakota began his research journey with a short article from *Time for Kids,* had slowly moved on to reading harder and harder material, and worked up to articles in *Life* and *National Geographic*!

Lesley's hope is that when students are faced with research projects or challenging textbook reading in junior high school, they'll take the extra time to find resources that they can read easily (fluently) and build background knowledge before tackling reading material that is just too hard. It was through the layering of texts, repetition of vocabulary, and time reading informational texts that students increased their fluency for reading in the content areas.

A Snapshot of Data

Spring Results of the Fourth-Grade Literacy Intervention Room (Fourteen Students)

Students in the fourth-grade literacy intervention room made great gains in the areas of reading with appropriate expression and phrasing (see Figure 7.4). Four students in the class improved from Partially Meets to Meets in all four components on the Oral Reading Fluency Scale. In the fall, 50 percent of the students fell below the standard for fluency rate compared with 28 percent of the students in the spring.

Figure 7.4

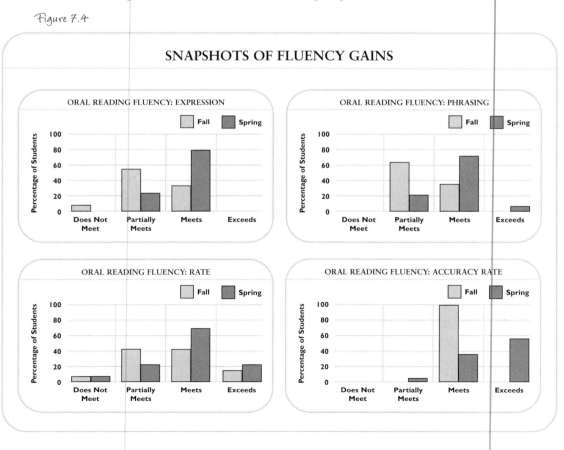

Reading rate is still an area in which students need to improve. The fact that students met the standard in the category of accuracy rate indicated that the teacher had chosen an appropriate passage to measure oral reading fluency (at the student's independent reading level). The data indicated that most of the students were reading fluently at their independent reading level. This is not to say all students were reading at grade-level expectations.

What We Learned

We think the most powerful aspect of the project was having the students watch themselves on tape as they read orally and set goals for themselves as readers. The video clips gave them a concrete visual model to examine the components of oral reading fluency. Students were quick to articulate what they needed to do to improve their fluency. The project built awareness of the components of fluency, and provided both students and teachers strategies to improve oral reading fluency and ultimately reading stamina.

An issue that surfaced during the project was the importance of appropriate book selection. Research by Allington shows that it is critical for students to be placed with appropriate books for instruction (95 percent accuracy rate) that are not too difficult (Allington 2000). Some of the students we taped had books that were too difficult. It is hard to measure reading fluency in that situation. It is also interesting to note that Gambrell, Wilson, and Gannt (1981) indicated that oral reading error rates of 5 percent or greater were linked to significant increases in off-task behavior (Allington 2000).

We plan to continue this project with the same pilot teachers next year, teaching them how to film their own students and expand it by inviting two new teachers to participate. We will make some changes. We are taping a few students we can use as models for our initial classroom presentation on fluency. We think that providing students with a visual model during the teaching session will help deepen their understanding of the components of reading fluency.

We want teachers more involved in the process. Hudson, Lane, and Pullen (2005) cite Zutell and Rasinski (1991) and note the importance of teachers needing to listen to their students read aloud and make judgments about their progress in reading fluency. Knowing this, we will ask classroom teachers to watch their own class VHS tape before the student self-assessment session and complete a running record on each of their students to gain insight into student reading behaviors. Teachers will also be expected to calculate the accuracy rate of the text reading. We hope by raising the awareness of accuracy rates that students will be better matched to literature and also given opportunities in the classroom to increase their reading stamina with extended text by reading books at their independent level.

Overall this was an energizing experience. It reminded us that if we plan to formally assess a concept, we need to be sure we are teaching it. The fluency awareness project highlights the importance of direct instruction, modeling, student practice, and involving students in the self-assessment process. It is also an example of how collaboration among staff can directly affect classroom instruction and spark school reform. As a result of this project, students and teachers have a greater awareness of what it means to be a fluent reader.

CHAPTER EIGHT

Support for Assessment

Evaluation ought to be one of the greatest energy givers for the teacher in the classroom. The best teachers evaluate from the time the first child enters the classroom until she leaves.

DONALD GRAVES

Suzanne, a fifth-grade teacher, took a leave of absence from school because of illness. She left in the spring before administering end-of-year assessments. I canceled plans, rearranged my schedule, and individually assessed all of her students in reading. I then guided the long-term substitute in completing the district spelling assessment and writing prompt. I scored, recorded, and filed all the student assessments in cumulative folders. I had not anticipated needing to complete assessments for teachers on leave, but by juggling responsibilities I was able to assist when the need arose.

The following spring, Sarah had to leave early on maternity leave because of complications with her pregnancy. Once again, I found myself digging through a teacher's classroom materials looking for what I would need to complete student assessments. I couldn't believe that only a year later I was in the same position from the previous spring— frantically changing plans so I could complete another set of classroom assessments.

Those first two springs set the pattern for every spring that has followed. Each March or April I have at least one, and sometimes two, teachers take unexpected and extended leaves of absence. I even joke with staff that we need a rule that nobody can have babies, adopt, or become ill during spring assessment time.

In addition to leaves of absence, teachers have resigned unexpectedly midway through the school year. In these cases, I have had to help write substitute plans, set up literature groups, figure out where the teacher left off in the curriculum, and support substitutes and newly hired teachers midyear as they got their feet on the ground.

Somewhere in my fourth year as literacy specialist, it hit me: part of my job has to include expecting the unexpected. Supporting classroom instruction when a teacher leaves unexpectedly is my responsibility as literacy specialist. Organizing for the unplanned assessments helped me to develop better assessment support for all teachers.

Literacy Curriculum and Assessment Notebooks

The literacy notebooks I've designed for all teachers are one solution to this issue of helping teachers develop core understandings and practices in curriculum and assessment, no matter when they begin work in the school. Every year teachers are faced with the daunting task of administering common literacy assessments to all their students. They are expected to formally assess their students in the fall (to inform instruction) and in the spring (for district evaluation purposes).

Every spring teachers asked questions about administering assessments. Even though we talked about assessment procedures, there was often confusion and misinterpretation. Adequate time for completing writing prompts was interpreted by some teachers as a onetime writing period of ninety minutes, whereas others had students taking the prompt through the writing process over several days. Even when I typed administering procedures for assessments, teachers often misplaced them. I can't tell you how many times we sat down to score student writing, only to have teachers fail to bring their writing rubrics. I became frustrated with copying and recopying the same materials for teachers. But the bigger issue was the inconsistency in how the literacy assessments were being administered to students.

In an effort to organize literacy assessments and to ensure validity and reliability of our local assessment system (and reduce my stress level), I worked with Rose Patterson, the K–2 literacy specialist, to develop notebooks filled with literacy materials all teachers would need. The notebooks outlined literacy expectations at each grade level. The red three-ring literacy binder stored literacy assessments, procedures for administering the assessments, scoring guidelines, benchmark papers, and end-of-year cumulative folder filing procedures. Each classroom teacher was provided with a literacy notebook. When teachers walked into scoring sessions empty-handed, I simply reminded them to get their literacy notebooks.

Teachers also use the notebooks to store student assessment information. When a teacher takes an unexpected leave, I am able to go into their classroom, find the red literacy notebook, and have immediate access to their classroom's student literacy information.

Literacy notebooks are updated at the start of every school year. New teachers entering the district are provided a literacy notebook, and appreciate it as an organizational tool. The literacy notebooks promote consistency in the administering of assessments, and have helped ensure the validity and reliability of our local literacy assessment system, regardless of who administers the assessment. Figure 8.1 shows the contents of the assessment notebooks used in grade 3.

Figure 8.1

CONTENTS OF GRADE 3 ASSESSMENT NOTEBOOKS

- Current classroom data
- Data sheet identifying targeted students working below grade-level expectations
- End-of-year filing procedures of literacy assessments
- Procedures for administering Developmental Reading Assessment (also resources for taking running records and analyzing student miscues)
- Procedures for administering and scoring district writing prompts
- Procedures for administering and interpreting spelling assessment
- Strategies to teach students to write constructed responses
- Local assessment: Patricia Polacco assessment
- Local assessment: Reflection on Writing—the revision assessment
- Third-grade curriculum

Preparing Student Assessment Materials

During assessment season I support teachers behind the scenes by helping to prepare student assessment materials. I copy and collate materials for the teachers. Every fall and spring I give each teacher a manila envelope that outlines the expectations and contains assessment materials for their class. I provide teachers with an outline of dates for administering assessments. This one-page outline is taped on the front of the assessment materials and shows how the administering of assessments is staggered throughout the first two months of school. The outline is optional, but the bottom line is that all fall data is due to me by the end of October. I have had positive feedback on the fall expectations outline that I provide teachers. Many teachers have shared that the time line helps them break down administering student assessments into manageable chunks, making the process less overwhelming. I repeat this once again in the spring, preparing assessment materials for teachers and providing an outline for spring assessment expectations. Fall assessment expectations for grade 3 are shown in Figure 8.2.

Why do I spend my time doing this? I do this so that teachers do not spend their precious time photocopying assessments. In his book *The Energy to Teach,* Donald Graves writes about energy drains such as the misuse of assessments. The purpose of administering a reading assessment to students is not simply to calculate reading levels, but rather to analyze the assessment to learn more about students' reading behaviors. It is our responsibility as educators to take the time to analyze and interpret the assessments that we give our students so that we can find out how we can individualize and tailor our instruction to meet their needs. I hope that by using my energy to help prepare materials for teachers, they can reserve their energy for the more important task of reviewing student assessments to inform their instruction.

Release Time for Administering Assessments

As a district we have also built in release time for teachers. Teachers are given a release day in the fall and spring to administer assessments to students without interruptions, with classroom coverage from substitutes. Release days are staggered so that adequate substitute coverage can be found. Teachers find empty spaces and quiet corners within the school to assess students during the day. The release time has helped alleviate the

FALL LITERACY ASSESSMENT EXPECTATIONS GRADE 3

Purpose

The purpose of administering fall literacy assessments is to determine instructional needs of students and to set student goals.

Materials

Student materials are copied for the whole class and are enclosed in the envelope.

Reading

Administer Developmental Reading Assessment (DRA) to students starting the week of September 12. See DRA Teacher Guide for procedures for administering DRA.

- Grade 3 Fall DRA Expectations

  Below Level 20

  At Level 24

  Above Level 34

- Record on literacy data sheet the level for beginning reading instruction.

Writing

- Administer the writing prompt week of September 5.

  —Bring writing prompts to scoring session.

  —Special education teachers, please give prompts back to classroom teachers.

- Scoring will be done September 16—early release day.

- Record independent developmental stage on literacy data sheet (Example: LB = Late Beginning).

Spelling

- Administer the Gentry Spelling Assessment week of September 19.

- The highest level, in which the student scores about 50 percent on a spelling list, is the approximate grade-level placement for instruction.

- Record the instructional spelling level on the literacy data sheet.

The purpose of collecting literacy data in the fall is to inform instruction and to use it as baseline data when comparing student growth over the year.

  Literacy data sheets due by October 14

Figure 8.2

burden of assessing students during a regular seat day where teachers try to fit assessments in around teaching.

I often spend time going over student assessments with teachers during the release days. We use the assessments to set instructional goals for students. Sometimes teachers want to go over the assessments for their whole class; other times teachers want to review a single assessment to gain another perspective on certain students. Reviewing assessments for the purpose of informing instruction is the most important part of the assessment process. I make sure I am available to staff and leave room in my schedule to meet with teachers.

New teachers often need support as they familiarize themselves with the district's assessment tools and interpret the results. For example, I recently reviewed spring assessments with a new teacher. The teacher reflected on her students' Developmental Reading Assessments and noted that all of them wrote poor summaries. As we talked more about this, she admitted that her students had few opportunities to write summaries in her classroom throughout the school year. We talked about ways that oral or written summaries could be incorporated into her reading workshop time or her content-area instruction. As a next step, I provided the teacher with resources that she could use to teach her students summarization. Reviewing her student assessments resulted in the teacher making the commitment to incorporate summarization into her classroom instruction.

I shared in Chapter 6 that while reviewing writing prompts with Cathy, a fifth-grade teacher, she questioned whether she provided students any concrete strategies to take on-demand writing assessments such as the district's fall and spring writing prompts. Cathy was not happy with her students' performance on the district's writing prompts, but admitted that she simply had her students write to the fall and spring prompt without having them produce on-demand writing during other times of the school year. As a result of this initial discussion, I worked with Cathy and other teachers to create a yearlong framework for introducing students to strategies for producing on-demand writing (see Chapter 6). After reviewing Cathy's writing data, I spent the next school year visiting her room once a month, working with her and her students on strategies for producing on-demand writing.

Another Set of Eyes

Throughout the year, I am asked to assess students in literacy. In these cases teachers want another perspective on a challenging student. Often the teacher thinks the student needs to be referred for further evaluation by the special education staff. In these cases I will work with the teacher and assess students they are concerned about before starting the referral

ISSUES AND RESOURCES CHART

These are issues that emerged in reviewing student assessments with teachers, as well as suggested resources.

Burning Issues	Suggested Resources
Reading Fluency	• *The Fluent Reader*, T. Rasinski • *Supporting Struggling Readers*, D. Strickland, K. Ganske, and J. Monroe
Summary Writing	• *Revisit, Reflect, Retell*, L. Hoyt • *Snapshots*, L. Hoyt • *Reciprocal Teaching at Work*, L. Oczkus
On-Demand Writing	• *The Author's Profile*, T. Beaver • *Teaching the Qualities of Writing Grades 3–6*, R. Fletcher and J. Portalupi • *Writing Through the Tween Years*, B. Morgan • *Better Answers*, A. Cole
Reading Comprehension	• *Strategies That Work*, S. Harvey and A. Goudvis • *Still Learning to Read*, F. Sibberson and K. Szymusiak
Word Study	• *Word Journeys*, K. Ganske • *Word Savvy*, M. Brand
Analyzing Oral Reading	• *Miscue Analysis Made Easy*, S. Wilde • *Running Records*, P. Johnston

Figure 8.3

process. In the beginning a few teachers took advantage of me by asking me to assess all the difficult students they were concerned about. I think they felt off the hook if the "literacy specialist" assessed the student of concern. It's taken me almost five years, but now I ask that the teacher pull together a history of interventions, identify their concerns to me, and show me the instructional strategies that they have tried before I administer any assessments to the student in question. After assessing a student, we meet to brainstorm instructional strategies that they can implement with the student. Sometimes having another set of eyes look at a student provides teachers with a fresh perspective on how to meet a student's learning needs.

During the winter, a third-grade teacher asked me to assess a student named Mary. The teacher was alarmed that Mary was reading at an instructional grade 2 reading level. Mary had been receiving one-to-one support (coordinated by the teacher) through Title I but was not making adequate gains. The teacher identified her as passive, struggling in the area of reading comprehension.

I assessed Mary using the Developmental Reading Assessment and Analytical Reading Assessment, and did a miscue analysis using the text from her literature group, *The Stories Julian Tells*. In reviewing Mary's assessments, I agreed that she was reading almost two years below grade-level expectations. One of Mary's weaknesses was in reading comprehension. The miscue analysis I did from her assigned literature book indicated that she was reading with only a 90 percent accuracy rate, and a slow reading rate of fewer than sixty words per minute. She made significant miscues that interfered with the comprehension of the text and attempted few self-corrections. I was concerned that Mary was being instructed in books that were just too hard for her to read. It was hard to determine if there was a learning issue, because there was no evidence that she had been placed with texts with which she had been successful. After meeting with the teacher and working with Mary, I too was concerned about Mary's limited progress but worried that it was a result of being placed in inappropriate texts all year. I recommended that Mary be discussed at a literacy team meeting.

Literacy Team Meetings

If a student continues to make limited progress, we hold a literacy team meeting about him or her. This meeting includes the classroom teacher, principal, a special education teacher, and a literacy specialist. We meet to review the student's cumulative folder, classroom performance, and current supports, and decide on next steps.

After reviewing Mary's literacy history and interventions to date, we decided that the special education teacher would work with her informally in a small group for the next six weeks. Mary would be placed with texts at her independent and instruction level so that we could focus on her weakness in the area of reading comprehension and her struggle to communicate what she knows about the books that she has read. She would focus specifically on strategies to help Mary identify her purpose for reading, and hold and communicate her thinking. The special education teacher and classroom teacher would work together to coordinate services.

Over the six weeks, each person would collect data on Mary's reading behaviors in the area of reading comprehension. The plan was to reconvene as a team and share our observations and identify strategies that worked with the student. If Mary was still not making progress, a referral would be written for further evaluation through special education.

At the end of six weeks we reconvened as a team. The special education teacher found that Mary was successful when taught one strategy at a time using a text that she could read with at least 95 percent accuracy. The special education teacher reported that Mary seemed engaged in her reading. She also brought evidence showing that Mary was successful in communicating her thinking when tasks were broken down into small chunks. Mary was able to use Post-its in the books to mark evidence in the text that she then used for her response to the text.

At the final literacy intervention meeting, we decided we would not refer Mary for evaluation, because gains were made in the six-week intervention. The strategies used could easily be replicated in the regular classroom and supported through supplemental Title I instruction. We documented for future teachers the importance of placing Mary with texts that were appropriate for her reading level, and that tasks need to be broken down into manageable parts for her to be successful.

Evaluating and Tracking Student Achievement

A system is in place to ensure that students do not fall through the cracks. Every fall and spring the principals and I meet with teachers individually to review their literacy data. The purpose of the meetings is to review class data and make sure that adequate support is in place for students not meeting grade-level expectations in reading and writing. Each teacher is scheduled for a thirty-minute meeting. We use a rotating substitute to provide coverage when we meet with teachers. See Figure 8.4 for some questions we use at literacy review meetings.

During these literacy meetings, teachers share their literacy assessment results and note observations in student performance. The school principal

Figure 8.4

PROMPT QUESTIONS FOR LITERACY REVIEW MEETINGS

- What are the strengths and needs of each student?
- What students are you concerned about?
- What students have made the most growth?
- What observations can you make about your overall literacy data?

facilitates the meetings. We use the teacher's literacy data sheet as the springboard for the meeting. We start at the top of the class and alphabetically work our way through the list, making sure we talk about each child's strengths and needs. As the teacher reflects on each student, the principal reviews the student's cumulative folder, the assistant principal listens and adds notes to the student's placement card that has already been filled out by the classroom teacher, and I take notes on students who are still at risk for literacy failure. I note students who are in the referral process, students who were referred during the year and did not qualify, and students who may still need to be referred in the future. I also reference my notes from the fall to make sure we followed through on students targeted in our October meeting.

Teachers also reflect on their class data as a whole. Teachers are quick to say if their class did poorly. An example of this is a teacher who had solid reading scores for her entire class but whose writing scores almost all fell in the does-not-meet category. There was a discrepancy between her strong reading scores and her poor writing scores. The teacher was disappointed, because one of her goals for the year was in the area of writing instruction. However, she recognized that writing instruction continued to be an area of weakness for her as reflected in her class literacy data, and she was committed to continuing work on improving writing instruction for her students.

The meetings provide a quick overview of the students in each class. I target students who are falling through the cracks and will continue to follow these students. The meetings are another check to ensure that student needs are being met. With more than four hundred fifty students in grades 3 through 5, it's impossible to micromanage the literacy needs of all the students on my caseload, but I can help track students over time and relay information about them from grade level to grade level and across buildings.

Tracking Student Achievement

Student literacy performance is tracked from kindergarten through fifth grade. Literacy information is maintained on a database.

The end of the year signals the collection, analyzing, and the reporting of our local literacy data for the school district K–5. I compile the results of the literacy data and write a yearly district literacy report. The literacy data is analyzed on a student, classroom, building, and district level. We break the data out into several subgroups. We track the cohorts of students who have been with our district since kindergarten and examine the performance of males versus females and free versus full-paying lunch students. The K–5 literacy report is shared with the district's leadership teams. The data is presented at the district's summer leadership retreat and is used to help set goals for the district in the area of literacy.

Supporting the Literacy Assessment Framework

Throughout the year I support the literacy assessment framework that the district has in place. However, the teacher ultimately is responsible for the day-to-day planning, instruction, and ongoing informal assessments and observations to ensure that student needs are being met. Teachers need to know their students. As a literacy specialist, I support teachers by maintaining consistency and organization in our literacy assessment system.

CHAPTER NINE

Scheduling and Budget

A schedule is a net for catching days.
ANNIE DILLARD

Ella, a curriculum coordinator in the district office, asked if I would chaperone during the school's career day for students. As organizer for the event, she was looking for warm, available, and no-cost substitutes to cover classrooms as outside speakers presented workshops to students.

I told her I couldn't commit to the day, because I was finishing up classroom work at another school and in the final stages of completing the literacy report for the district. I would have loved being part of the event with the staff and students, but I was swamped in data analysis and working against time to finish projects.

It wasn't the first time that I've been asked by a teacher to cover a classroom, and I know it will not be the last. Because I don't have a set schedule, my time is sometimes perceived as "unstructured" and "available." I am grateful to have supportive administrators who allow me to create my own schedule. They remind me that one of my most important jobs is to plan my time well, protecting it to ensure I meet goals set over months and years. At the same time, I need to be flexible about time, to meet important literacy needs that emerge every day with the teachers and children I

serve.

A Typical Day

I have the flexibility to create my own schedule, and I thrive on a well-planned day. Before I leave at the end of each day, I sketch out my schedule for the following day. Having a plan helps me prioritize projects and maximize my time. The backbone of my daily schedule is my time in Carolyn and Lesley's literacy intervention classrooms each morning. This part of my schedule is sacred.

Next I write in times that I am working with other teachers. In addition to the literacy rooms I usually work in two other classrooms during the day. Finally, I plug in projects I need to complete in empty blocks of time. When not in classrooms, I prep for classroom work, organize study group materials, work on curriculum, and plan for upcoming presentations.

Although I try to be responsive to teachers' needs, I work them in around my scheduled times of working in the literacy rooms, teachers that I am currently coaching or assisting, and my preset study group meeting times.

Many days I never get to the "other" list of projects that I hoped to work on during my day. Even with the best-laid plans and intentions, unexpected meetings, phone calls, and new tasks have a way of creeping in.

At the end of each day I reflect on what I actually accomplished and record the day in my daily planner. The planner documents how I spent the day and gives me a concrete visual illustration of how I used my time. This daily ritual is important to me because so much of my day is not tangible. At the beginning of a day it looks like I have chunks of free time, but at the end of the day after I fill in the unexpected chats and needs, I usually find that I used every bit of time available. Figure 9.1 is a sample of a typical day.

What's in a Week

The weekdays always pass quickly, and before I know it, I am once again at the end of another week. Friday is the one day of the week that I am not in classrooms. It's a day to complete unfinished projects, assist and guide technicians, and meet with administrators. It's also the day that literacy intervention meetings are scheduled. This is the one day of the week that I can scrape together larger chunks of uninterrupted time.

Over the course of any given week I have worked in two schools, facilitated two teacher study groups, met with Rose the K–2 literacy specialist, met with administrators, and worked in eight different classrooms as part of ongoing coaching and support. Figure 9.2 shows a typical week for me.

TYPICAL DAY IN NOVEMBER

Time	Place	What This Means
7:00–8:30	Available for teachers in literacy room	I was available to help teachers gather materials. I also talked with a teacher about some new ideas she had.
8:30–9:15	Inclusive support in Carolyn's grade 4 literacy intervention room	I worked in Carolyn's room for forty-five minutes during writer's workshop. I presented a mini-lesson on revising lead sentences.
9:15–10:00	Inclusive support in Lesley's grade 5 literacy intervention room	I worked in Lesley's room for forty-five minutes. Lesley led a mini-lesson on revising line breaks in poetry. I conferred with students during writing workshop.
10:00–10:45	Flexible time (new-student screening)	This was time that I was not committed to being in a classroom. I used this time to screen a new student.
10:45–11:30	Partnership with master teacher on writing in classroom	I worked with Cathy in her room during writing workshop.
11:30–12:15	Lunch	I ate a sandwich as I read e-mail. I still blocked out a lunch period even if I didn't take it.
12:15–1:00	Flexible time (finished new-student screening)	I finished writing up the notes on the new student I screened earlier in the morning. I passed notes on to the classroom teacher and principal.
1:00–1:45	Worked in new teacher's classroom	I worked with Paige, a new teacher, on reading workshop. We had worked during the year to establish multiple literature groups in her room. I often worked with a small literature group during my time in her room.
1:45–2:30	Flexible time	Cathy came to the literacy room and we had an "unplanned" chat and debriefed about the writer's workshop from the morning. We also planned what she would work on during the week with students before I returned.
2:30–3:00	Prep for classroom work	I reviewed my schedule for the next day and made sure that all materials for my classroom work were prepared. I recorded my day in my daily planner. I then set up for the after-school study group.
3:00–4:00	Study group in the literacy room	I facilitated a teacher study group on strategic reading.
4:00–4:30	Literacy room	I cleaned up from the study group. I stayed around for teachers who wanted to talk more.

Figure 9.1

17 Monday	* Start day at Mitchell School Thursday 20
7:30—8:15 Word Study	7:00—8:00 Available for teachers
8:25 Prep for day	8:00—8:30 Coffee with technicians
8:30—9:15 Carolyn's room	8:30—9:15 Observe student in Title I group
9:15—10:00 Lesley's room	9:15—10:00 Meet with Rose
10:00—10:45 Jill's room: fluency project lesson	10:00—11:00 Lucy's room: writing
10:45—11:30 Next steps for study group:	11:00—11:45 Lunch
reflection morning	Travel back to Hall School
11:30—12:15 Lunch	12:00—12:45
12:30—1:15 Donna's room: "My Life in Seven	12:45—1:30 Writing group with students
Stories" — leads	1:30—2:30 Prep study group
1:15 Organize purchase orders/prep for family	3:00—4:00 Strategic reading #2 (study group)
literacy breakfast for 10/18	
18 Tuesday	**Friday 21**
7:00—8:30 Available for teachers/prep for day	7:00—8:00 Available for teachers/set up
8:30—9:15 Carolyn's room	8:00—10:00 Technician in-service
9:15—10:00 Lesley's room	10:00—10:45 Meet with Carolyn and Lesley:
10:00—10:45	debrief in literacy intervention room
10:45 Travel to Mitchell School/Lunch	10:45—11:30 Reflect on morning in-service/plan
11:30—12:15 Mary's room: reading workshop	for next Monday
12:30—1:30 Lucy's room: writing	11:30—12:15 Lunch
1:30 Travel/set up at Mt. Merici Catholic School	12:15—1:00 Literacy intervention meeting (Josh)
2:00—3:00 Mt. Merici staff meeting	1:00—1:30 Meeting with Harriet (principal)
	1:30—2:00
	2:00—3:00 Writing group with students
19 Wednesday	**Saturday 22**
7:00—8:30 Available for teachers	* Highlighted times are priority and other projects
8:30—9:15 Carolyn's room (intervention room)	fit around these times
9:15—10:00 Lesley's room (intervention room)	
10:00—10:45 New student screening	
10:45—11:30 Writing in Cathy's room (Gr. 5)	
11:30—12:15 Lunch	**Sunday 23**
12:15—1:00 Finish new student screening	
1:00—1:45 Reading in Paige's room (Gr. 4)	
1:45—2:30 Debriefing with Cathy (unplanned)	
2:30—3:00 Set up study group	
3:00—4:00 Study group: strategic reading #1	

Figure 9.2
A Typical Week

Overview of a Month

Every month has a sense of predictability. I sketch out the overview of every month on a calendar. This enables me to see the bigger picture of what I need to get done during the month. I plot all the presentations, meetings, and family literacy events. I know that every month I have to prepare for our school's staff meeting, a presentation at a local Catholic school in Waterville, workshops with Title I technicians, and organizing resources for six teacher study groups. Depending on the time of year I might also have a district staff event and family literacy breakfast to plan. It's also safe to say that at least once a month I am pulled out of the district to attend a conference or state-sponsored meeting. Figure 9.3 shows a typical month for me.

Figure 9.3
Overview of a
Month

Sunday	Monday	Tuesday	Wednesday	Thursday	Friday	Saturday
						1
2	3	4 *Grade 3 study group (revision)*	5	6 *District In-service 1/2 day Grade 3 teachers*	7 *In-service In-service technicians 8:00—10:00*	8
9	10 *No school*	11	12 *Staff meeting*	13 *Study group: strategic reading #1*	14 *Literacy data due!*	15
16	17 *Word study study group*	18 *Mt. Merici staff meeting*	19	20 *Study group: strategic reading #2*	21	22
23	24	25	26	27	28 *Study group — full day Portfolio release 7:15—8:30 literacy breakfast Lynne*	29
30	31					

Rhythm of a Year

Over the last five years I have found that the year takes on its own rhythm. My busiest time as literacy specialist is in the beginning of the school year as I start up literacy services and organize Title I support, and the end of the year when I am immersed in data analysis and attempting to bring closure to one year while preparing for the upcoming year. The job is circular and never ending.

August and September

The work that I do at the end of the summer and in September tends to be organizational in nature. It is a busy, high-pressure time. My goal in the beginning of the year is to complete new-student screenings, order professional resources, update the literacy database with new student information, distribute literacy folders to teachers, organize family literacy activities, and complete necessary curriculum work so that I can start working in classrooms to support teachers by the beginning of October.

October–May: Supporting Teachers

From October to mid-May I reserve most of my time for staff development and supporting teachers in their classrooms. I try to keep paperwork, data analysis, and the development of local assessments to a minimum so that it doesn't interrupt and interfere with my classroom work. During this time I facilitate study groups, support teachers in their classrooms, and work in the literacy intervention rooms, with a daily schedule much like the one in Figure 9.1. I also develop new resources and find materials for teachers. If I have extra time, I plug away at assessment mandates that have come my way relentlessly.

June: Data Analysis and Planning Ahead

Once June comes, I pull out of classrooms, including the literacy intervention rooms. This is the time of year that I outline budget needs, do calendar work for the upcoming year, plan and organize Summer Literacy Jump Start for the literacy intervention classrooms, and collect and analyze year-end literacy data.

Budget

Every spring I develop a budget based on current and planned staff development. I work with Rose, the K–2 literacy specialist, to review our needs and propose a budget to the administration that will support literacy needs for both students and teachers.

Literacy specialists in other districts marvel at the videos, books, and supplies that I have available for teachers. Some have even asked to borrow videos so that they can use them with their teachers. Not long ago I had a conversation with Tonya, a literacy specialist for another district. She wanted to know how I got the money to buy the books and videos. Even though she was the Title I coordinator and managed Title IA funds, she didn't know she could take money out of these funds for professional resources and supplies.

Title money is available for professional resources. However, many districts use up most of their Title money for staffing salaries, or they buy professional resources at the last minute in the spring, without a plan for how to use them. They simply don't want to lose the money at the end of the year. I have actually had personnel from other districts call me during the last week of June, asking what I would recommend that they buy because they have $10,000 they have to spend before the end of the month.

Allocating money for professional resources is a priority. I would argue that spending $3,500 for study groups that will benefit more than twenty-five teachers over the course of a year will have a greater effect on learning than the $3,000 plus travel expenses that a district will spend for a famous big shot to come do a one-hour kick-off-the-year keynote presentation.

We are not a rich school, and we too run into financial predicaments. This spring Rose and I met with administrators to look at next year's anticipated staffing and budget needs. We did not have enough money to cover existing needs and proposed new positions. Typical of most schools, we too talked about cutting supplies lines. But Rose and I argued that the $3,500 proposed for study groups and teacher supplies such as books for their classrooms was a small investment compared with the nearly $25,000 it would cost to add another position. You would have to cut a lot of lines to come up with that kind of money. We argued to preserve the supplies for teachers, the very resources that support them in their learning and change initiatives. The administrators quickly backed us and decided that they would cut the proposed positions before shaving off the money allocated for study groups and professional resources.

We are lucky to have administrators who support this philosophy of teacher development and understand that it requires some investment of funds, and they back us up with the bucks.

What money is needed to support students and teachers in their literacy learning? This is the question I ponder yearly as I reflect on my budgetary requests for the upcoming year. I have worked with a yearly budget of as little as $2,000, and as much as $32,000 to support literacy in grades 3 through 5. Both amounts are a very small portion of the near-million dollars that the district receives in Title monies from federal grants.

When thinking about budgetary requests, I slot the needs into the categories of instructional support, professional development, parent involvement, and summer school. Under these headings I plug in our literacy initiatives that support both teacher and student learning. See Figure 9.4 for a sample budget.

Figure 9.4

SAMPLE LITERACY BUDGET GRADES 3–5

Parent Involvement—$4,050

- **Family Literacy Breakfasts at Albert S. Hall School $2,800**
  —author fees, food, books, supplies
- **Parent Resources—$250**
  We subscribe to *Reading Connections,* a monthly publication that focuses on family involvement in literacy. It is copied and sent home to parents.
  —subscription, copying paper
- **Family Involvement for Intervention Classrooms—$1,000**
  Families from Carolyn and Lesley's room are invited into the classrooms for writing celebrations and to view student portfolios.
  —food, supplies, transportation

Instructional Support—$12,900

- **Title I Supplies $500**
  This includes supplies for Title I literacy technicians and materials for the literacy room.
  —highlighters, Post-its, paper, journals, etc.
- **Classroom Libraries—$5,400**
  Each teacher receives a $200 purchase order at the start of the school year to buy books at a local bookstore as a means to update and maintain classroom libraries.
- **Multiple Copies for School Literacy Collection—$3,000**
  Money is set aside to purchase replacement books and new books for our multiple-copy library. All teachers have access to these books.
- **Curriculum and Assessment Materials—$2,000**
  This money is used to fund the printing of the end-of-year literacy report, assessment materials, and the replacement of assessment materials.

continued

- **Book Swap Program, Albert S. Hall School—$2,000**

  This money is used to purchase books for the student book swap. The idea is to get accessible and appealing books in the hands of kids (see Chapter 2).

Professional Development—$10,000

- **Professional Books/Professional Videos—$2,000**

  Money is set aside to purchase new professional books and videos to add to the professional library in the literacy room.

- **Materials for Professional Development at Staff Meetings—$300**

  We choose one professional book as our staff book. This book is explored and discussed at monthly staff meetings. The money is used to purchase these books for teachers.

- **Study Groups—$3,500**

  This money is set aside to support study groups. The money is used to purchase materials, books, food, and supplies that teachers may ask for as the groups go through the year.
  —books, professional videos, supplies, food, journals

- **Professional Memberships for Buildings—$200**

  The school has memberships to the National Council for Teachers of English (NCTE) and the International Reading Association (IRA). This gives teachers easy access to updated professional journals (*Language Arts* and *The Reading Teacher*). I also subscribe to *Book Links* for new book ideas.

- **Workshops Teachers—$2,000**

  This money is set aside for classroom teachers to attend literacy conferences that may come up during the year. We have also used this money to have teachers attend national conferences such as that of the National Council of Teachers of English.

- **Workshops, Jen (NCTE)—$1,000**

  I usually attend a national conference for my personal professional development. I put professional development money allotted for me toward this one conference experience.

- **Workshops Educational Technician III—$1,000**

  We take our Title I technicians on a two-day retreat to a local hotel. The first day is a reflective day of reading and discussing. The second day technicians attend the Mid-Maine Title I conference that is at the same location.

Summer School—$5,000

- **Summer Literacy Jump Start, Albert S. Hall School—$5,000**

  This runs the week before school starts. It is designed to get students back in the daily routines of reading and writing (see Chapter 5).
  —teacher salaries, transportation, snacks, supplies

  Total budget: $31,950 out of Title IA

Figure 9.4 continued

Calendar Work

I work with the building principals and K–2 literacy specialist on the school calendars before the end of the school year. I provide each principal with dates for study group meetings, family literacy breakfasts, and in-services that have been scheduled for the upcoming year. Dates are provided ahead of time to avoid scheduling conflicts within the school and between buildings. Because administrators work on the master calendar during the summer, I try to be one step ahead and get the literacy dates on the calendar first. K–5 is housed in two different schools (K–3 and 4–5), so it is important that we create a K–5 calendar that works for families with children in both schools.

Planning Summer Literacy Jump Start

Summer Literacy Jump Start (see Chapter 5) was designed as an opportunity to give students a jump start for the school year and to get back into the daily routines of reading and writing. In addition to implementing this with our literacy intervention classrooms we have expanded the program for students entering first through fifth grade. Summer Literacy Jump Start is organized in June. Selected students are invited to participate, transportation plans are set, purchase orders are prepared, and teachers are hired to teach at the different grade levels. The program is set up before leaving for the summer. Teachers run the classrooms the week before students return to school for the year.

Evaluating and Tracking Student Achievement

The end of the year also signals the collection, analysis, and reporting of our local literacy data for the school district K–5 (see Chapter 8). Once teachers complete spring assessments, they turn their class data in to me. Data is entered into the database. The results of the literacy data are compiled into a K–5 literacy report. The literacy data is analyzed on the student, classroom, building, and district level. The K–5 literacy report is then shared at the summer leadership retreat. The cycle of planning continues and another school year begins! See Figure 9.5 to see how we plan a typical year.

A YEAR OF PLANNING

August	• **Summer Leadership Retreat** Our school district holds a two-day summer retreat. This retreat includes the district's leadership team. During this retreat we review local and state data and set school and district goals for the upcoming year. • **Organizational Details** I return to work a week before the official start of the school year. I finalize Title I support schedules, run off and organize assessment materials for teachers, prepare purchase orders, and update literacy notebooks.
September	• **Organizing Title I Support Services** I work with Rose, K–2 literacy specialist, to get Title I support services started. • **New-Student Screenings** All new students need to be screened. We usually have approximately 25 new students entering our district the first week of school in grades 3 through 5. I work with the Title I technicians to administer literacy assessments to new students. • **Order Professional Resources** Fall is a great time to discover new professional publications. I put together orders for professional books that will support the district's literacy learning. • **Planning for Family Involvement Activities** We start the year in October with a family literacy breakfast, one of two we hold during the year. In September, I confirm the guest author, place food orders, and create literacy resource folders for each family to take home.
October–May	• **Supporting Teachers in the Classroom** The bulk of my time is devoted to supporting teachers in the classroom. I spend approximately half of each day in classrooms with students and teachers. • **Weekly Meetings with Administrators** The purpose of the weekly meeting with administrators is to reflect on the needs on the schools and plan in-services. Meeting also helps to ensure consistency in literacy practices within grades and between buildings. • **Weekly Meetings with Rose, K–2 Literacy Specialist** Rose and I meet weekly to review Title I literacy needs and plan in-services. Meeting ensures consistency in literacy practices between grade levels and schools.

Figure 9.5

- **In-services at Staff Meetings**

  I prepare for in-services at our monthly staff meetings.

- **Monthly Study Groups**

  I prepare and set up for the six study groups that are held each month.

- **Monthly In-Service with Technicians**

  We have monthly in-services with our Title I technicians. I set aside time each month to plan and organize resources.

- **Attend a National Conference**

  For my own professional development I attend an annual literacy conference. I tend to go to the annual convention of the National Council for Teachers of English or the annual convention for the International Reading Association.

June

- **Planning Study Groups for Upcoming Year**

  Study groups are organized for the upcoming school year.

- **Calendar Work**

  Dates are set aside for study group meetings, teacher assessment days, and in-services with technicians.

- **Budget**

  Literacy needs are outlined and new budgets are proposed to administration for upcoming year.

- **Planning Summer Literacy Jump Start**

  Summer Literacy Jump Start is organized for August.

- **Evaluating and Tracking Student Achievement**

  Student data is collected, reviewed, and analyzed. A district K–5 literacy report is written.

Figure 9.5
continued

A New School Year, New Stories: A Wave from the Heart

What I can't capture in describing how I plot my hours, days, weeks, and months are the moments that mean the most to me. I remember one of these moments well. It was a sunny September afternoon. The first week of school was almost complete. It was the end of the day when Officer Main, the policeman assigned to our school patrol, came to see me. He told me I needed to go look at my car, because someone had just backed into it. I walked with him down the hallway thinking that this was not in my plans for the day. I wanted a hassle-free afternoon, because I was heading to Vermont with my family right after school.

As I approached the car, I noticed my windshield wipers were up. This was a typical "wave from the heart" from Carolyn. At that moment I knew I had been tricked. I looked at my car and then heard giggles and laughter from above. "1 . . . 2 . . . 3 . . . Gotcha" called out Carolyn's students, who were lined up against the library windows, looking down at me as I examined my car.

My car was covered in photographs of the students. They had taped their pictures on the windows. Carolyn had neatly taped herself to the passenger seat next to me. My windshield wipers were up, and a big purple ribbon was tied to the back windshield wiper.

I couldn't help but smile. The students had a great sense of humor, and Carolyn had truly pulled one over on me. I was proud to be part of the class and to be included in such a great prank. I knew that this moment next to my car, with Carolyn's students watching my reaction from above, would become one of our "stories" as we ventured into another new school year together.

I drove home that Friday afternoon with a big smile—and of course with all the student photographs taped to my windows, and the big purple ribbon tied to the back of my car, my own parade.

These stories, these connections that I make with teachers and kids around literacy, mean the most to me. I've shared my thinking as one emerging literacy leader as best I could. Although I spend my days implementing strategies for literacy learning, my favorite moments are still those when colleagues and kids share their stories—their hearts—with one another.

Appendix

Mentor Texts for Teaching Comprehension

Picture books are a great tool to explicitly teach comprehension strategies. They tend to be short and are effective models for teaching various comprehension strategies. They can be used as springboards for class discussions or as the foundation for a think-aloud. When I select mentor texts, I look for books that will serve as strong examples for the comprehension strategies that I want to teach. Titles in bold are from original bins; other titles were added over time.

Making Connections

I look for books with subject matter and story lines in which students can easily make connections (text to self, text to world, text to text).

Bang, Molly. 1999. *When Sophie Gets Angry—Really, Really Angry*. New York: Blue Sky.

Cooney, Barbara. 1991. *Roxaboxen*. New York: Scholastic.

DiSalvo-Ryan, Dyanne. 1991. *Uncle Willie and the Soup Kitchen*. New York: Morrow Junior Books.

Ehrlich, Amy, ed. 1996. *When I Was Your Age: Original Stories About Growing Up*. Cambridge: Candlewick.

Fletcher, Ralph. 1998. *Flying Solo*. New York: Clarion.

———. 1997. ***Ordinary Things: Poems from a Walk in Early Spring*. New York: Atheneum Books for Young Readers.**

———. 1995. *Fig Pudding*. New York: Bantam.

Fox, Mem. 1985. *Wilfrid Gordon McDonald Partridge*. New York: Miller.

Frasier, Debra. 2000. *Miss Alaineus: A Vocabulary Disaster*. San Diego: Harcourt Brace Jovanovich.

Graves, Donald. 1996. *Baseball, Snakes, and Summer Squash: Poems About Growing Up*. Honesdale, PA: Wordsong.

Henkes, Kevin. 2000. *Wemberly Worried*. New York: Greenwillow.

———. 1990. *Julius the Baby of the World*. New York: Trumpet.

Houston, Gloria. 1992. *My Great-Aunt Arizona*. New York: Scholastic.

Kimmel, Elizabeth Cody. 2004. *My Penguin Osbert*. Cambridge: Candlewick.

Laminack, Lester. 2004. *Saturdays and Teacakes*. Atlanta: Peachtree.

Lichtenheld, Tom. 2003. *What Are You So Grumpy About?* New York: Little, Brown.

Lithgow, John. 2000. *The Remarkable Farkle McBride*. New York: Simon & Schuster.

Little, Jean. 1986. *Hey World, Here I Am!* New York: HarperTrophy.

MacLachlan, Patricia. 1994. *All the Places to Love*. New York: HarperCollins.

Palatini, Margie. 2000. *Bedhead*. New York: Scholastic.

Plourde, Lynn. 2002. *School Picture Day*. New York: Dutton Children's Books.

Polacco, Patricia. 2002. *When Lightning Comes in a Jar*. New York: Philomel.

———. 1998. *Thank You, Mr. Falker*. New York: Scholastic.

———. 1994. *My Rotten Redheaded Older Brother*. New York: Aladdin.

———. 1991. *Some Birthday!* New York: Simon & Schuster.

Rylant, Cynthia. 1985. *The Relatives Came*. New York: Scholastic.

———. 1982. *When I Was Young in the Mountains*. New York: E. P. Dutton.

Seinfeld, Jerry. 2002. *Halloween*. Boston: Little, Brown.

Viorst, Judith. 2001. *Super-Completely and Totally the Messiest*. New York: Atheneum.

———. 1972. *Alexander and the Terrible, Horrible, No Good, Very Bad Day*. New York: Scholastic.

Visualization

To teach visualization, I look for books that paint pictures in the reader's mind through the author's use of vivid language.

Aliki. 1998. *Spoken Memories*. New York: Greenwillow.

Baylor, Byrd. 1986. *I'm in Charge of Celebrations*. New York: Charles Scribner.

Benton, Jim. 2003. *Franny K. Stein, Mad Scientist*. New York: Aladdin.

Brinkloe, Julie. 1985. *Fireflies*. New York: Aladdin.

Cameron, Ann. 1981. *The Stories Julian Tells*. New York: Bullseye.

Dorros, Arthur. 1991. *Abuela*. New York: Dutton Children's Books.

Dragonwagon, Crescent. 1990. *Home Place*. New York: Scholastic.

Fletcher, Ralph. 1997. *Twilight Comes Twice*. New York: Clarion.

———. 1997. *Ordinary Things: Poems from a Walk in Early Spring*. New York: Atheneum Books for Young Readers.

Hoffman, Alice. 1997. *Fireflies a Winter Tale.* New York: Scholastic.
London, Jonathan. 1999. *Puddles.* New York: Puffin.
———. 1998. *Dream Weaver.* New York: Silver Whistle.
Mazer, Anne. 1991. *The Salamander Room.* New York: Dragonfly.
Mowat, Farley. 1961. *Owls in the Family.* New York: Bantam Skylark.
Plourde, Lynn. 1999. *Wild Child.* New York: Aladdin.
Rylant, Cynthia. 1995. *The Van Gogh Café.* New York: Scholastic.
———. 1982. *When I Was Young in the Mountains.* New York: E. P. Dutton.
Singer, Marilyn. 1994. *Turtle in July.* New York: Aladdin.
Worth, Valerie. 1987. *All the Small Poems.* New York: Farrar, Straus & Giroux.
Zolotow, Charlotte. 1992. *The Seashore Book.* New York: HarperCollins.

Important Ideas

It is important for students to be able to identify the important ideas of a story. I find that nonfiction books work well. I also choose stories with topics that students might be less familiar with. It forces them to think about what they are reading and to sift through information to make meaning of the story.

Adkins, Jan. 2004. *What If You Met a Pirate?* Brookfield, CT: Roaring Brook.
Avi. 2003. *Silent Movie.* New York: Atheneum Books for Young Readers.
Bridges, Ruby. 1999. *Through My Eyes.* New York: Scholastic.
Collard, Sneed. 1998. *Animal Dazzlers: The Role of Brilliant Colors in Nature.* New York: Franklin Watts.
Farris, Christine King. 2003. *My Brother Martin.* New York: Scholastic.
Golenbock, Peter. 1990. *Teammates.* San Diego: Harcourt Brace Jovanovich.
Harwood, Lynne. 1994. *Honeybees at Home.* Gardiner, ME: Tilbury House.
Hooper, Meredith. 2000. *River Story.* Cambridge: Candlewick.
Patterson, Dr. Francine. 1999. *Koko-Love! Conversations with Koko.* New York: Dutton Children's Books.
Polacco, Patricia. 2003. *The Graves Family.* New York: Philomel.
———. 2001. *Mr. Lincoln's Way.* New York: Scholastic.
———. 1992. *Chicken Sunday.* New York: Paper Star Book.
———. 1992. *Mrs. Katz and Tush.* New York: Dell.
Shetterly, Susan. 1999. *Shelterwood.* Gardiner, ME: Tilbury House.
Silver, Donald. 1993. *One Small Square Backyard.* New York: W. H. Freeman.
St. George, Judith. 2002. *So You Want to Be an Inventor?* New York: Philomel.
Woodson, Jacqueline. 2001. *The Other Side.* New York: G. P. Putnam's Sons.

Asking Questions

In finding mentor texts to teach the comprehension strategy of asking questions, I look for books that evoke wonderings in students.

Abercrombie, Barbara. 1995. *Charlie Anderson.* New York: Aladdin.

Baylor, Byrd. 1975. *The Desert Is Theirs.* New York: Aladdin.

Bunting, Eve. 2000. *Swan in Love.* New York: Atheneum.

———. 1999. *Going Home.* Boston: Houghton Mifflin.

———. 1991. *Fly Away Home.* New York: Clarion.

———. 1990. *The Wall.* New York: Clarion.

———. 1989. *The Wednesday Surprise.* New York: Trumpet.

Cronin, Doreen. 2003. *Diary of a Worm.* New York: Joanna Cotler.

Fleishman, Paul. 1993. *Bull Run.* New York: HarperTrophy.

Frasier, Debra. 2000. *Miss Alaineus: A Vocabulary Disaster.* San Diego: Harcourt Brace Jovanovich.

Greenfield, Eloise. 1978. *Honey I Love.* New York: Crowell.

Heide, Florence Parry, and Judith Heide Gilliland. 1990. *The Day of Ahmed's Secret.* New York: Scholastic.

Hughes, Langston. 1994. *The Dream Keeper and Other Poems.* New York: Knopf.

Madonna. 2003. *Mr. Peabody's Apples.* New York: Callaway.

Mochizuki, Ken. 1993. *Baseball Saved Us.* New York: Lee and Low.

Nye, Naomi Shihab. 1996. *This Same Sky.* New York: Aladdin.

Polacco, Patricia. 2003. *The Graves Family.* New York: Philomel.

———. 1994. *Pink and Say.* New York: Philomel.

Pringle, Laurence. 1997. *An Extraordinary Life: The Story of a Monarch Butterfly.* New York: Scholastic.

Rylant, Cynthia. 1995. *The Van Gogh Café.* San Diego: Harcourt Brace Jovanovich.

———. 1988. *All I See.* New York: Orchard.

Van Allsburg, Chris. 1986. *The Stranger.* Boston: Houghton Mifflin.

Drawing Inferences

When teaching students to understand inferences, I tell them to read like a detective and to look for clues the author has left between the pages of the book to support their process of making meaning of the story. I look for books that lend themselves to strong class discussions.

Brinkloe, Julie. 1985. *Fireflies.* New York: Aladdin.

Bunting, Eve. 1991. *Fly Away Home.* New York: Clarion.

———. 1988. *How Many Days to America?* New York: Clarion.

Golenbock, Peter. 1990. *Teammates.* San Diego: Harcourt Brace Jovanovich.

Polacco, Patricia. 1995. *Babushka's Doll.* New York: Aladdin.

Ringgold, Faith. 1991. *Tar Beach.* New York: Scholastic.

Schertle, Alice. 1994. *How Now, Brown Cow?* New York: Browndeer.

Van Allsburg, Chris. 2002. *Zathura.* Boston: Houghton Mifflin.

———. 1993. *The Sweetest Fig.* Boston: Houghton Mifflin.

———. 1992. *The Widow's Broom.* Boston: Houghton Mifflin.

———. 1990. *Just a Dream*. Boston: Houghton Mifflin.
———. 1988. *Two Bad Ants*. Boston: Houghton Mifflin.
Wargin, Kathy-jo. 2000. *The Legend of the Loon*. Chelsea, MI: Sleeping Bear.
Weisner, David. 1991. *Tuesday*. New York: Scholsatic.

Synthesizing Information

When choosing books to teach the strategy of synthesizing information I look for ones that force the reader think throughout the story. To gain understanding of the author's intent the reader must work beyond a literal interpretation of the text.

Abercrombie, Barbara. 1995. *Charlie Anderson*. New York: Aladdin.
Babbit, Natalie. 1975. *Tuck Everlasting*. New York: Farrar, Straus & Giroux.
Baylor, Byrd. 1994. *The Table Where Rich People Sit*. New York: Aladdin.
Bourgeois, Paulette. 2001. *Oma's Quilt*. Toronto: Kids Can.
Bunting, Eve. 1994. *Smoky Night*. San Diego: Voyager.
Coles, Robert. 1995. *The Story of Ruby Bridges*. New York: Scholastic.
Hathorn, Libby. 1994. *Way Home*. New York: Crown.
Lobel, Arnold. 1980. *Fables*. New York: Harper & Row.
Muth, Jon. 2002. *The Three Questions Based on a Story by Leo Tolstoy*. New York: Scholastic.
Pallotta, Jerry. 2000. *Dory Story*. Watertown, MA: Talewinds.
Pinkney, Andrea. 2003. *Fishing Day*. New York: Hyperion.
Plourde, Lynn. 2003. *Summer's Vacation*. New York: Simon & Schuster.
———. 2002. *Spring's Sprung*. New York: Simon & Schuster.
———. 2001. *Winter Waits*. New York: Simon & Schuster.
———. 1999. *Wild Child*. New York: Aladdin.
Polacco, Patricia. 2001. *Betty Doll*. New York: Philomel.
Ringgold, Faith. 1991. *Tar Beach*. New York: Scholastic.
Silverstein, Shel. 1964. *The Giving Tree*. New York: Harper & Row.
Van Allsburg, Chris. 2002. *Zathura*. Boston: Houghton Mifflin.
———. 1995. *Bad Day at River Bend*. Boston: Houghton Mifflin.
———. 1993. *The Sweetest Fig*. Boston: Houghton Mifflin.
———. 1992. *The Widow's Broom*. Boston: Houghton Mifflin.
———. 1991. *The Wretched Stone*. Boston: Houghton Mifflin.
———. 1990. *Just a Dream*. Boston: Houghton Mifflin.
———. 1988. *Two Bad Ants*. Boston: Houghton Mifflin.
———. 1984. *Mysteries of Harris Burdick*. Boston: Houghton Mifflin.
———. 1983. *The Wreck of the Zephyr*. Boston: Houghton Mifflin.
———. 1981. *Jumanji*. Boston: Houghton Mifflin.
Wiesner, David. 1999. *Sector 7*. New York: Clarion.
Willems, Mo. 2003. *Don't Let the Pigeon Drive the Bus!* New York: Hyperion.
Wisniewski, David. 1996. *Golem*. New York: Clarion.
Yolen, Jane. 1988. *The Devil's Arithmetic*. New York: Trumpet.

Mentor Texts for Teaching the Craft of Writing

Many of the books listed here as mentor texts are on multiple lists and can be used to teach various aspects of writing craft. A good book goes a long way. I encourage teachers to find a handful of books to use as mentor texts, and use them with their students over and over again. The purpose of a mentor text is to move beyond the comprehension of the story and dissect the book for its writing craft. Books that were in my first version of the bins are in bold; those added later are in plain text.

Creating Characters

These books have strong and believable characters. The characters in the selected mentor texts come alive to the reader through their actions, gestures, and or dialog.

Brisson, Pat. 1998. *The Summer My Father Was Ten.* Honesdale, PA: Boyds Mills.
Bunting, Eve. 1997. *On Call Back Mountain.* New York: Scholastic.
Cameron, Ann. 1981. *The Stories Julian Tells.* New York: Random House.
Coles, Robert. 1995. *The Story of Ruby Bridges.* New York: Scholastic.
Cooney, Barbara. 1996. *Eleanor.* New York: Viking.
———. 1988. *Miss Rumphius.* New York: Puffin.
Demi. 2001. *Gandhi.* New York: Margaret McElderry.
DiTerlizzi, Tony. 2002. *The Spider and the Fly.* New York: Simon & Schuster.
Duncan, Alice Faye. 1999. *Miss Viola and Uncle Ed.* New York: Simon & Schuster.
Falconer, Ian. 2000. *Olivia.* New York: Simon & Schuster.
Fenner, Carol. 1995. *Yolanda's Genius.* New York: McElderry.
Fleischman, Paul. 1999. *Weslandia.* Cambridge: Candlewick.
Fletcher, Ralph. 2000. *Grandpa Never Lies.* New York: Clarion.
———. 1995. *Fig Pudding.* New York: Bantam.
Gantos, Jack. 2003. *What Would Joey Do?* New York: HarperTrophy.
Gantos, Jack. 2000. *Joey Pigza Loses Control.* New York: HarperTrophy.
Giff, Patrica Reilly. 2002. *Pictures of Hollis Woods.* New York: Wendy Lamb.
Golenbock, Peter. 1990. *Teammates.* San Diego: Harcourt Brace Jovanovich.
Greenfield, Eloise. 1978. *Honey I Love.* New York: Crowell.
Hannigan, Katherine. 2004. *Ida B . . . and Her Plans to Maximize Fun, Avoid Disaster, and (Possibly) Save the World.* New York: Greenwillow.
Henkes, Kevin. 1998. *Chester's Way.* New York: Scholastic.
———. 1996. *Lilly's Purple Plastic Purse.* New York: Greenwillow.
Hoose, Phillip. 1998. *Hey, Little Ant.* New York: Scholastic.
Houston, Gloria. 1992. *My Great-Aunt Arizona.* New York: Scholastic.
Krull, Kathleen. 1996. *Wilma Unlimited.* San Diego: Harcourt Brace Jovanovich.

Lithgow, John. 2000. *The Remarkable Farkle McBride*. New York: Simon & Schuster.

MacLachlan, Patricia. 1985. *Sarah, Plain and Tall*. New York: Trumpet.

———. 1980. *Arthur for the Very First Time*. New York: Harper & Row.

Martin, Jacquine Briggs. 1998. *Snowflake Bentley*. Boston: Houghton Mifflin.

McDonald, Megan. 1995. *Insects Are My Life*. New York: Orchard.

Napoli, Donna Jo. 2001. *Albert*. New York: Simon & Schuster.

Patterson, Katherine. 1978. *The Great Gilly Hopkins*. New York: Harper & Row.

Pochocki, Ethel. 1989. *Rosebud and Red Flannel*. Camden, ME: Down East.

Roberts, Lynn. 2003. *Rapunzel: A Groovy Fairy Tale*. New York: Abrams.

Ryan, Pam Munoz. 2002. *When Marian Sang*. New York: Scholastic.

———. 1999. *Amelia and Eleanor Go for a Ride*. New York: Scholastic.

Spinelli, Eileen. 2001. *Sophie's Masterpiece*. New York: Simon & Schuster.

Steptoe, John. 1989. *Mufaro's Beautiful Daughters*. New York: Scholastic.

Van Allsburg, Chris. 1993. *The Sweetest Fig*. Boston: Houghton Mifflin.

———. 1992. *The Widow's Broom*. Boston: Houghton Mifflin.

———. 1990. *Just a Dream*. Boston: Houghton Mifflin.

Crafting Beginning, Middle, and End

These books have a strong story structure to teach beginning, middle, and end. The stories appeal to students in grades 3–5. I look for stories that can be easily plotted out on a graphic organizer to examine the structure of the story.

Brisson, Pat. 1998. *The Summer My Father Was Ten*. Honesdale, PA: Boyds Mills.

Bunting, Eve. 1999. *Going Home*. Boston: Houghton Mifflin.

Cameron, Ann. 1981. *The Stories Julian Tells*. New York: Random House.

Cheng, Andrea. 2002. *When the Bees Fly Home*. Gardiner, ME: Tilbury House.

Cooney, Barbara. 1994. *Only Opal*. New York: Putnam & Grossett.

———. 1988. *Miss Rumphius*. New York: Puffin.

Cronin, Doreen. 2004. *Duck for President*. New York: Simon & Schuster.

———. 2002. *Diary of a Worm*. New York: Joanna Cotler.

DiSalvo-Ryan, DyAnne. 1991. *Uncle Willie and the Soup Kitchen*. New York: William Morrow.

DiTerlizzi, Tony. 2002. *The Spider and the Fly*. New York: Simon & Schuster.

Fletcher, Ralph. 2000. *Grandpa Never Lies*. New York: Clarion.

———. 1998. *Flying Solo*. New York: Clarion.

Friedman, Ina. 1984. *How My Parents Learned to Eat*. Boston: Houghton Mifflin.

Fox, Mem. 1985. *Wilfrid Gordon McDonald Partridge*. New York: Miller.

Gantos, Jack. 2003. *What Would Joey Do?* New York: HarperTrophy.

Gerstein, Mordicai. 2003. *The Man Who Walked Between the Towers*. New York: Scholastic.

Golenbock, Peter. 1990. *Teammates.* San Diego: Harcourt Brace Jovanovich.

Henkes, Kevin. 1998. *Chester's Way.* New York: Scholastic.

Hoose, Phillip. 1998. *Hey, Little Ant.* New York: Scholastic.

Johnson, Angela. 2004. *Just Like Josh Gibson.* New York: Simon & Schuster.

Laminack, Lester. 2004. *Saturdays and Teacakes.* Atlanta: Peachtree.

McDonald, Megan. 1995. *Insects Are My Life.* New York: Orchard.

Napoli, Donna Jo. 2001. *Albert.* New York: Simon & Schuster.

Perrow, Angeli. 1988. *Captain's Castaway.* Camden, ME: Down East.

Plourde, Lynn. 2004. *The First Feud Between the Mountain and the Sea.* Camden, ME: Down East.

Pochocki, Ethel. 1989. *Rosebud and Red Flannel.* Camden, ME: Down East.

Polacco, Patricia. 1992. *Chicken Sunday.* New York: Paper Star.

———. 1992. *Mrs. Katz and Tush.* New York: Bantam.

Silverstein, Shel. 1964. *The Giving Tree.* New York: Harper & Row.

Spinelli, Eileen. 2001. *Sophie's Masterpiece.* New York: Simon & Schuster.

Van Allsburg, Chris. 1993. *The Sweetest Fig.* Boston: Houghton Mifflin.

———. 1992. *The Widow's Broom.* Boston: Houghton Mifflin.

———. 1990. *Just a Dream.* Boston: Houghton Mifflin.

Crafting Endings

I look for books that show students that there are different ways to end stories. I want students to make a conscious decision about how they are going to leave their reader at the end of their writing—with a circular, surprise, emotional, connect title, or ambiguous ending.

Brisson, Pat. 1998. *The Summer My Father Was Ten.* Honesdale, PA: Boyds Mills.

Bunting, Eve. 1997. *Ducky.* New York: Clarion.

———. 1989. *The Wednesday Surprise.* New York: Trumpet.

Cameron, Ann. 1981. *The Stories Julian Tells.* New York: Random House.

Cronin, Doreen. 2000. *Click, Clack, Moo: Cows That Type.* New York: Scholastic.

Demi. 1991. *The Artist and the Architect.* New York: Henry Holt.

DiTerlizzi, Tony. 2002. *The Spider and the Fly.* New York: Simon & Schuster.

Falconer, Ian. 2003. *Olivia . . . and the Missing Toy.* New York: Atheneum.

Fletcher, Ralph. 2000. *Grandpa Never Lies.* New York: Clarion.

———. 1995. *Fig Pudding.* New York: Bantam.

Fox, Mem. 1985. *Wilfrid Gordon McDonald Partridge.* New York: Miller.

Funke, Cornelia. 2005. *Pirate Girl.* New York: Scholastic.

Golenbock, Peter. 1990. *Teammates.* San Diego: Harcourt Brace Jovanovich.

Haseley, Dennis. 2002. *A Story for Bear.* San Diego: Silver Whistle.

Hoose, Phillip. 1998. *Hey, Little Ant.* New York: Scholastic.

Irving, John. 2004. *A Sound Like Someone Trying Not to Make a Sound.* New York: Random House.

McDonald, Megan. 1995. *Insects Are My Life*. New York: Orchard.
Oram, Hiawyn. 1998. *Just Dog*. New York: Scholastic.
Pallotta, Jerry. 2000. *Dory Story*. Watertown, MA: Talewinds.
Pilkey, Dav. 2004. *The Paperboy*. New York: Scholastic.
Pochocki, Ethel. 1989. *Rosebud and Red Flannel*. Camden, ME: Down East.
Provencher, Rose-Marie. 2004. *Slithery Jake*. New York: HarperCollins.
Roberts, Lynn. 2003. *Rapunzel: A Groovy Fairy Tale*. New York: Abrams.
Rylant, Cynthia. 1987. *Silver Packages: An Appalachian Christmas Story*. New York: Scholastic.
———. 1982. *When I Was Young in the Mountains*. New York: E. P. Dutton.
Say, Allen. 1993. *Grandfather's Journey*. Boston: Houghton Mifflin.
Shannon, George. 1989. *Sea Gifts*. Boston: David R. Godine.
Silverstein, Shel. 1964. *The Giving Tree*. New York: Harper & Row.
Spinelli, Eileen. 2001. *Sophie's Masterpiece*. New York: Simon & Schuster.
Van Allsburg, Chris. 1993. *The Sweetest Fig*. Boston: Houghton Mifflin.
———. 1992. *The Widow's Broom*. Boston: Houghton Mifflin.
———. 1990. *Just a Dream*. Boston: Houghton Mifflin.
———. 1991. *The Wretched Stone*. Boston: Houghton Mifflin.
———. 1981. *Jumanji*. Boston: Houghton Mifflin.
———. 1979. *The Garden of Abdul Gasazi*. Boston: Houghton Mifflin.
Woodson, Jacqueline. 2004. *Going on Home Soon*. New York: G. P. Putnam's Sons.
Woodson, Jacqueline. 2001. *The Other Side*. New York: G. P. Putnam's Sons.

Crafting Voice

Teaching voice is all about finding books that talk to the reader. I find the best way to teach the concept of voice is through read-aloud. Students often recognize voice through the author's use of language. Students identify voice when they hear it through powerful read-alouds.

Arnold, Ted. 2004. *Even More Parts*. New York: Dial Books for Young Readers.
———. 1997. *Parts*. New York: Dial.
Buehner, Caralyn. 2004. *Superdog: The Heart of a Hero*. New York: HarperCollins.
Cole, Joanna. 1992. *The Magic Schoolbus on the Ocean Floor*. New York: Scholastic.
Dahl, Roald. 1974. *Danny, the Champion of the World*. New York: Knopf.
Falconer, Ian. 2000. *Olivia*. New York: Simon & Schuster.
Greenfield, Eloise. 1978. *Honey I Love and Other Love Poems*. New York: Trumpet.
Heide, Florence Parry. 2000. *Some Things Are Scary*. Cambridge: Candlewick.
Henkes, Kevin. 1996. *Lilly's Purple Plastic Purse*. New York: Greenwillow.
———. 1990. *Julius the Baby of the World*. New York: Trumpet.
Jennings, Patrick. 1996. *Faith and the Electric Dogs*. New York: Scholastic.

Kirk, David. 1995. *Miss Spider's Wedding.* New York: Scholastic.
Madonna. 2003. *The English Roses.* New York: Callaway.
Palatini, Margie. 1995. *Piggie Pie.* New York: Clarion.
Paterson, Katherine. 1978. *The Great Gilly Hopkins.* New York: Harper & Row.
Roberts, Lynn. 2003. *Rapunzel: A Groovy Fairy Tale.* New York: Abrams.
Scieszka, Jon. 1989. *The True Story of the 3 Little Pigs.* New York: Scholastic.
Seinfeld, Jerry. 2002. *Halloween.* Boston: Little, Brown.
Solheim, James. 1998. *It's Disgusting and We Ate It! True Food Facts from Around the World Throughout History.* New York: Simon & Schuster.
Stanley, Diane. 2003. *Goldie and the Three Bears.* New York: HarperCollins.
Viorst, Judith. 1972. *Alexander and the Terrible, Horrible, No Good, Very Bad Day.* New York: Scholastic.
Willis, Jeanne. 1988. *Earthlets.* New York: Puffin Unicorn.

Crafting Leads

Ralph Fletcher refers to leads as "opening the door." Just as in teaching endings, I try to find books that demonstrate different ways for students to think about leading readers into their stories.

Austin, Heather. 2002. *Visiting Aunt Sylvia's.* Camden, ME: Down East.
Cannon, Janell. 1993. *Stellaluna.* San Diego: Harcourt Brace Jovanovich.
Cooney, Barbara. 1988. *Island Boy.* New York: Penguin.
Dahl, Roald. 1991. *The Minpins.* New York: Puffin.
Fletcher, Ralph. 2000. *Grandpa Never Lies.* New York: Clarion.
Greenburg, Dan. 1997. *The Zack Files: I'm Out of My Body Please Leave a Message.* New York: Grossett and Dunlap.
Jenkins, Steve. 1998. *Hottest, Coldest, Deepest.* Boston: Houghton Mifflin.
Krull, Kathleen. 1996. *Wilma Unlimited.* San Diego: Harcourt Brace Jovanovich.
Lithgow, John. 2000. *The Remarkable Farkle McBride.* New York: Simon & Schuster.
McKissack, Patricia. 1988. *Mirandy and Brother Wind.* New York: Trumpet.
Munson, Derek. 2000. *Enemy Pie.* San Francisco: Chronicle.
Polacco, Patricia. 1995. *Babushka's Doll.* New York: Aladdin.
————. 1990. *Just Plain Fancy.* New York: Trumpet.
Provensen, Alice, and Martin Provensen. 1983. *The Glorious Flight Across the Channel with Louis Bleriot.* New York: Viking.
Rylant, Cynthia. 1997. *The Blue Hill Mountains.* San Diego: Harcourt Brace Jovanovich.
————. 1991. *Night in the Country.* New York: Aladdin.
Scieszka, Jon. 1989. *The True Story of the 3 Little Pigs.* New York: Scholastic.
Solheim, James. 1998. *It's Disgusting and We Ate It! True Food Facts from Around the World Throughout History.* New York: Simon & Schuster.

Crafting Titles

Titles are important because they are the first thing that draws a reader to a book. I try to find examples of titles that evoke wonderings and invite the reader to open up the book.

Arnold, Ted. 1997. *Parts.* **New York: Dial.**
Baylor, Byrd. 1975. *The Desert Is Theirs.* **New York: Aladdin.**
Bedard, Michael. 1999. *The Clay Ladies.* New York: Tundra.
Brisson, Pat. 1998. *The Summer My Father Was Ten.* Honesdale, PA: Boyds Mills.
Bunting, Eve. 1994. *Smokey Night.* **San Diego: Harcourt Brace Jovanovich.**
Calmenson, Stephanie. 1994. *Rosie, a Visiting Dog's Story.* New York: Scholastic.
Cannon, Janell. 2000. *Crickwing.* San Diego: Harcourt Brace Jovanovich.
Fenner, Carol. 1995. *Yolanda's Genius.* **New York: McElderry.**
Fletcher, Ralph. 1995. *Fig Pudding.* **New York: Bantam.**
Golenbock, Peter. 1990. *Teammates.* **San Diego: Harcourt Brace Jovanovich.**
Harris, Robie. 2004. *Don't Forget to Come Back!* Cambridge: Candlewick.
Heide, Florence Parry, and Judith Heide Gilliland. 1990. *The Day of Ahmed's Secret.* **New York: Scholastic.**
Jeffers, Susan. 1991. *Brother Eagle, Sister Sky.* **New York: Scholastic.**
Houston, Gloria. 1992. *My Great-Aunt Arizona.* **New York: Scholastic.**
Krull, Kathleen. 1996. *Wilma Unlimited.* **San Diego: Harcourt Brace Jovanovich.**
LaMarche, Jim. 2000. *The Raft.* New York: HarperCollins.
Munson, Derek. 2000. *Enemy Pie.* San Francisco: Chronicle.
Polacco, Patricia. 1998. *My Rotten Redheaded Older Brother.* **New York: Aladdin.**
————. 1992. *Chicken Sunday.* New York: Paper Star.
Ringgold, Faith. 1991. *Tar Beach.* **New York: Crown.**
Say, Allen. 2004. *Music for Alice.* Boston: Houghton Mifflin.
Shannon, George. 1989. *Sea Gifts.* **Boston: David R. Godine.**
Spinelli, Eileen. 2001. *Sophie's Masterpiece.* New York: Simon & Schuster.
Van Allsburg, Chris. 1991. *The Wretched Stone.* **Boston: Houghton Mifflin.**
Van Laan, Nancy. 1989. *Rainbow Crow.* **New York: Dragonfly.**

Crafting Setting

It is important for students to embed a setting within their writing. I look for books that communicate a sense of place.

Bunting, Eve. 1997. *On Call Back Mountain.* **New York: Scholastic.**
Cameron, Ann. 1981. *The Stories Julian Tells.* **New York: Random House.**
Cannon, Janell. 2000. *Crickwing.* San Diego: Harcourt Brace Jovanovich.
Fletcher, Ralph. 2003. *Hello Harvest Moon.* New York. Clarion.

———. 1997. *Twilight Comes Twice*. New York: Clarion.
Funke, Cornelia. 2005. *Pirate Girl*. New York: Scholastic.
Hesse, Karen. 1997. *Out of the Dust*. New York: Scholastic.
Hest, Amy. 1997. *When Jessie Came Across the Sea*. Cambridge, MA: Candlewick.
Hoban, Russell. 1999. *The Sea-thing Child*. Cambridge: Candlewick.
MacLachlan, Patricia. 1985. *Sarah, Plain and Tall*. New York: Trumpet.
———. 1980. *Arthur for the Very First Time*. New York: Harper & Row.
Rylant, Cynthia. 1987. *Birthday Presents*. New York: Orchard.
———. 1983. *Appalachia: The Voices of Sleeping Birds*. San Diego: Harcourt
    Brace Jovanovich.
Wells, Rosemary. 2002. *Wingwalker*. New York: Hyperion.
Williams, Sherley Anne. 1992. *Working Cotton*. New York: Trumpet.

Crafting with Words

Words paint pictures in readers' minds. Word choice is a powerful tool to
a writer. I want students to recognize that words can bring a book alive for
their readers. I look for mentor texts that demonstrate the effective use of
language through word choice.

Arnold, Ted. 2004. *Even More Parts*. New York: Dial Books for Young Readers.
Brennan, Herbie. 2001. *Frankenstella*. New York: Bloomsbury.
Brisson, Pat. 1998. *The Summer My Father Was Ten*. Honesdale, PA: Boyds
    Mills.
Cannon, Janell. 2004. *Pinduli*. New York: Scholastic.
Fletcher, Ralph. 2003. *Hello Harvest Moon*. New York: Clarion.
———. 1997. *Twilight Comes Twice*. New York: Clarion.
Frasier, Debra. 2000. *Miss Alaineus: A Vocabulary Disaster*. San Diego: Harcourt
    Brace Jovanovich.
Funke, Cornelia. 2005. *Pirate Girl*. New York: Scholastic.
George, William. 1992. *Winter at Long Pond*. New York: William Morrow.
Hoberman, Mary. 2002. *Right Outside My Window*. New York: Mondo.
Howell, Will. 1999. *I Call It Sky*. New York: Walker.
Lindbergh, Reeve. 1993. *Grandfather's Lovesong*. New York: Puffin.
Palatini, Margie. 2003. *The Perfect Pet*. New York: HarperCollins.
———. 1995. *Piggie Pie*. New York: Clarion.
**Pilkey, Dav. 1994. *Dog Breath: The Horrible Trouble with Hally Tosis*. New
    York: Blue Sky.**
Plourde, Lynn. 2003. *Summer's Vacation*. New York: Simon & Schuster.
———. 2002. *Spring's Sprung*. New York: Simon & Schuster.
———. 2001. *Winter Waits*. New York: Simon & Schuster.
———. 1999. *Wild Child*. New York: Aladdin.
Provencher, Rose-Marie. 2004. *Slithery Jake*. New York: HarperCollins.
Rohmann, Eric. 1997. *The Cinder-Eyed Cats*. New York: Dragonfly.
Ryan, Pam Munoz. 2002. *When Marian Sang*. New York: Scholastic.

Scieszka, Jon, and Lane Smith. 2001. *Baloney (Henry P.)*. New York: Viking.
Singer, Marilyn. 2003. *How to Cross a Pond: Poems About Water*. New York: Knopf.
Stevenson, Harvey. 2003. *Looking at Liberty*. New York: HarperCollins.
Waldman, Neil. 1999. *The Starry Night*. Honesdale, PA: Boyds Mills.
Warnock-Kinsey, Natalie. 1989. *The Canada Geese Quilt*. New York: Yearling.
Wells, Rosemary. 1993. *Waiting for the Evening Star*. New York: Dial Books for Children.
Yolen, Jane. 1987. *Owl Moon*. New York: Scholastic.

Original Mentor Texts for Crafting "Characters"	Mentor Texts Added Over the Last Few Years
Fig Pudding, Ralph Fletcher	*When Marian Sang*, Pam Muñoz Ryan
Sarah, Plain and Tall, Patricia MacLachlan	*Grandpa Never Lies*, Ralph Fletcher
The Stories Julian Tells, Ann Cameron	*Hey, Little Ant*, Phillip Hoose
Tar Beach, Faith Ringgold	*Insects Are My Life*, Megan McDonald
Honey I Love, Eloise Greenfield	*When I Was Your Age: Original Stories About Growing Up*, Edited by Amy Ehrlich
The Great Gilly Hopkins, Katherine Patterson	*Gandhi*, Demi
Wilma Unlimited, Kathleen Krull	*Rosebud and Red Flannel*, Ethel Pochocki
Yolanda's Genius, Carol Fenner	*The Sweetest Fig*, Chris Van Allsburg
Teammates, Peter Golenbock	*Just a Dream*, Chris Van Allsburg
Amelia and Eleanor Go for a Ride, Pam Muñoz Ryan	*Eleanor*, Barbara Cooney
Chester's Way, Kevin Henkes	*Sophie's Masterpiece*, Eileen Spinelli
Mufaro's Beautiful Daughters, John Steptoe	*The Race*, Caroline Repchuk
Miss Rumphius, Barbara Cooney	*Olivia*, Ian Falconer
My Great-Aunt Arizona, Gloria Houston	*The Spider and the Fly*, Tony DiTerlizzi
	Miss Viola and Uncle Ed Lee, Alice Faye Duncan
	Albert, Donna Jo Napoli
	Superdog: The Heart of a Hero, Caralyn Buehner
	Amber Was Brave, Essie Was Smart, Vera B. Williams
	Ida B . . . and Her Plans to Maximize Fun, Avoid Disaster, and (Possibly) Save the World, Katherine Hannigan
	What Would Joey Do?, Jack Gantos

Professional Books

It is important to support the professional development of teachers through new professional resources. Our professional library offers the latest publications in the area of literacy.

Allen, J. 2004. *Tools for Teaching Content Literacy.* Portland, ME: Stenhouse.

———. 2000. *Yellow Brick Roads: Shared and Guided Paths to Independent Reading 4–12.* Portland, ME: Stenhouse.

———. 1999. *Words, Words, Words: Teaching Vocabulary in Grades 4–12.* Portland, ME: Stenhouse.

Allen, J., and K. Gonzalez. 1997. *There's Room for Me Here: Literacy Workshop in the Middle School.* Portland, ME: Stenhouse.

Allen, J., B. Michalove, and B. Shockley. 1993. *Engaging Children: Community and Chaos in the Lives of Young Literacy Learners.* Portsmouth, NH: Heinemann.

Allington, R. L. 2000. *What Really Matters for Struggling Readers: Designing Research-Based Programs.* New York: Longman.

Anderson, C. 2000. *How's It Going? A Practical Guide to Conferring with Student Writers.* Portsmouth, NH: Heinemann.

Angelillo, J. 2003. *Writing About Reading: From Book Talk to Literary Essays, Grades 3–8.* Portsmouth, NH: Heinemann.

———. 2002. *A Fresh Approach to Teaching Punctuation: Helping Young Writers Use Conventions with Precision and Purpose.* New York: Scholastic.

Almasi, J. 2002. *Teaching Strategic Processes in Reading.* New York: Guilford Press.

Austin, T. 1994. *Changing the View: Student-Led Parent Conferences.* Portsmouth, NH: Heinemann.

Atwell, N. 1998. *In the Middle: New Understanding About Writing, Reading, and Learning.* Portsmouth, NH: Heinemann.

Baker, L., M. J. Dreher, and J. Guthrie, eds. 2000. *Engaging Young Readers: Promoting Achievement and Motivation.* New York: Guilford Press.

Balajthy, E., and S. Lipa-Wade. 2003. *Struggling Readers: Assessment and Instruction in Grades K–6.* New York: Guilford Press.

Bear, D., M. Invernizzi, S. Templeton, and F. Johnston. 2003. *Words Their Way: Study for Phonics, Vocabulary, and Spelling Instruction in Grades 4–12.* Upper Saddle River, NJ: Prentice Hall.

Beaver, T. 1998. *The Author's Profile: Assessing Writing in Context.* Portland, ME: Stenhouse.

Beck, I., M. McKeown, R. Hamilton, and L. Kucan. 1997. *Questioning the Author: An Approach for Enhancing Student Engagement with Text.* Newark, DE: International Reading Association.

Beers, K. 2002. *When Kids Can't Read, What Teachers Can Do: A Guide for Teachers 6–12.* Portsmouth, NH: Heinemann.

Brand, M. 2004. *Word Savvy: Integrated Vocabulary, Spelling, and Word Study Grades 3–6.* Portland, ME: Stenhouse.

Calkins, L. 2001. *The Art of Teaching Reading.* New York: Longman.

———. 1990. *Living Between the Lines.* Portsmouth, NH: Heinemann.

———. 1986. *The Art of Teaching Writing.* Portsmouth, NH: Heinemann.

Chandler, K., and the Mapleton Teacher-Research Group. 1999. *Spelling Inquiry: How One School Caught the Mnemonic Plague.* Portland, ME: Stenhouse.

Cole, A. D. 2002. *Better Answers: Written Performance That Looks Good and Sounds Smart.* Portland, ME: Stenhouse.

Collins, K. 2004. *Growing Readers: Units of Study in the Primary Classroom.* Portland, ME: Stenhouse.

Daniels, H. 2002. *Literature Circles: Voice and Choice in Book Clubs and Reading Groups.* 2nd ed. Portland, ME: Stenhouse.

———. 2001. *Looking into Literature Circles* (videotape). Portland, ME: Stenhouse.

Daniels, H., and M. Bizar. 2004. *Teaching the Best Practice Way: Methods That Matter, K–12.* Portland, ME: Stenhouse.

Davies, A. 2000. *Making Classroom Assessment Work.* Merville, BC: Connections Publishing.

Davis, J., and S. Hill. 2003. *The No-Nonsense Guide to Teaching Writing: Strategies, Structure, and Solutions.* Portsmouth, NH: Heinemann.

Duthie, C. 1996. *True Stories: Nonfiction Literacy in the Primary Classroom.* Portland, ME: Stenhouse.

Evans, K. 2001. *Literature Discussions in the Intermediate Grades: Dilemmas and Possibilities.* Newark, DE: International Reading Association.

Fletcher, R. 1996. *Breathing In, Breathing Out: Keeping a Writer's Notebook.* Portsmouth, NH: Heinemann.

———. 1996. *A Writer's Notebook: Unlocking the Writer Within You.* New York: Avon.

———. 1993. *What a Writer Needs.* Portsmouth, NH: Heinemann.

Fletcher, R., and J. Portalupi. 2004. *Teaching the Qualities of Writing Grades 3–6.* Portsmouth, NH: Heinemann.

———. 2002. *When Students Write* (videotape). Portland, ME: Stenhouse.

———. 1998. *Craft Lessons: Teaching Writing K–8.* Portland, ME: Stenhouse.

Fountas, I. C., and G. S. Pinnell. 2000. *Guiding Readers and Writers (Grades 3–6): Teaching Comprehension, Genre, and Content Literacy.* Portsmouth, NH: Heinemann.

Ganske, K. 2000. *Word Journeys: Assessment-Guided Phonics, Spelling, and Vocabulary Instruction.* New York: Guilford Press.

Gentry, R. 2004. *The Science of Spelling: The Explicit Specifics That Make Great Readers and Writers (and Spellers!).* Portsmouth, NH: Heinemann.

———. 1997. *My Kid Can't Spell: Understanding and Assisting Your Child's Literacy Development.* Portsmouth, NH: Heinemann.

Glazer, S., and C. Brown. 1993. *Portfolios and Beyond: Collaborative Assessment in Reading and Writing.* Norwood: MA: Christopher Gordon.

Graves, D. 1994. *A Fresh Look at Writing.* Portsmouth, NH: Heinemann.

———. 1991. *Build a Literate Classroom.* Portsmouth, NH: Heinemann.

Graves, D., and B. Sunstein, eds. 1992. *Portfolio Portraits.* Portsmouth, NH: Heinemann.

Hahn, M. 2002. *Reconsidering Read-Aloud.* Portland, ME: Stenhouse.

Hansen, J. 1987. *When Writers Read.* Portsmouth, NH: Heinemann.

Harvey, S. 1998. *Nonfiction Matters: Reading, Writing, and Research in Grades 3–8.* Portland, ME: Stenhouse.

Harvey, S., and A. Goudvis. 2003. *Think Nonfiction! Modeling Reading and Research* (videotape). Portland, ME: Stenhouse.

———. 2000. *Strategies That Work: Teaching Comprehension to Enhance Understanding.* Portland, ME: Stenhouse.

Heard, G. 2002. *The Revision Toolbox: Teaching Techniques That Work.* Portsmouth, NH: Heinemann.

———. 1999. *Awakening the Heart: Exploring Poetry in the Elementary and Middle School.* Portsmouth, NH: Heinemann.

Heffernan, L. 2004. *Critical Literacy and Writer's Workshop: Bringing Purpose and Passion to Student Writing.* Newark: DE: International Reading Association.

Hill, B., N. Johnson, and K. Noe. 1995. *Literature Circles and Response.* Norwood, MA: Christopher Gordon.

Hindley, J. 1996. *In the Company of Children.* Portland, ME: Stenhouse.

Hoyt, L. 2003. *Navigating Informational Texts* (videotape). Portsmouth, NH: Heinemann.

———. 2001. *Snapshots: Literacy Minilessons Up Close.* Portsmouth, NH: Heinemann.

———. 1998. *Revisit, Reflect, Retell: Strategies for Improving Reading Comprehension.* Portsmouth, NH: Heinemann.

Hubbard, R., and B. Power. 1993. *The Art of Classroom Inquiry: A Handbook for Teacher-Researchers.* Portsmouth, NH: Heinemann.

Hughes, M., and D. Searle. 1997. *The Violent E and Other Tricky Sounds: Learning to Spell from Kindergarten Through Grade 6.* Portland, ME: Stenhouse.

Keene, E. O., and S. Zimmermann. 1997. *Mosaic of Thought: Teaching Comprehension in a Reader's Workshop.* Portsmouth, NH: Heinemann.

Johnston, P. 2000. *Running Records: A Self-Tutoring Guide.* Portland, ME: Stenhouse.

Lane, B. 1993. *After the End: Teaching and Learning Creative Revision.* Portsmouth, NH: Heinemann.

Lyons, C. 2003. *Teaching Struggling Readers: How to Use Brain-based Research to Maximize Learning.* Portsmouth, NH: Heinemann.

Marshall, J. 2002. *Are They Really Reading? Expanding SSR in the Middle Grades.* Portland, ME: Stenhouse.

McMackin, M., and Siegel, B. 2002. *Knowing How: Researching and Writing Nonfiction 3–8.* Portland, ME: Stenhouse.

Miller, D. 2002. *Reading with Meaning: Teaching Comprehension in the Primary Grades.* Portland, ME: Stenhouse.

———. 2002. *Happy Reading! Creating a Predictable Structure for Joyful Teaching and Learning* (videotape). Portland, ME: Stenhouse.

Moline, S. 1995. *I See What You Mean: Children at Work with Visual Information.* Portland, ME: Stenhouse.

Morgan, B., with D. Odom. 2004. *Writing Through the Tween Years: Supporting Writers, Grades 3–6.* Portland, ME: Stenhouse.

Nagy, W. 1988. *Teaching Vocabulary to Improve Reading Comprehension.* Newark, DE: International Reading Association.

New Standards. 1999. *Reading Grade by Grade and Writing: Primary Literacy Standards for Kindergarten Through Third Grade.* Pittsburgh: National Center on Education and the Economy and the University of Pittsburgh.

Newkirk, T. 2002. *Misreading Masculinity: Boys, Literacy, and Popular Culture.* Portsmouth, NH: Heinemann.

Oczkus, L. 2004. *Super 6 Comprehension Strategies: 35 Lessons and More for Reading Success.* Norwood, MA: Christopher Gordon.

———. 2003. *Reciprocal Teaching at Work: Strategies for Improving Reading Comprehension.* Newark: DE: International Reading Association.

Opitz, M., and T. V. Rasinski. 1998. *Good-Bye Round Robin: 25 Effective Oral Reading Strategies.* Portsmouth, NH: Heinemann.

Portalupi, J., and R. Fletcher. 2003. *Talking About Writing* (videotape). Portland, ME: Stenhouse.

———. 2001. *Nonfiction Craft Lessons: Teaching Informational Writing K–8.* Portland, ME: Stenhouse.

Power, B. 1996. *Taking Note: Improving Your Observational Notetaking.* Portland, ME: Stenhouse.

Ray, K. W. 2002. *What You Know by Heart: How to Develop Curriculum for Your Writing Workshop.* Portsmouth, NH: Heinemann.

———. 1999. *Wondrous Words: Writers and Writing in the Elementary Classroom.* Urbana, IL: National Council of Teachers of English.

Ray, K. W., and L. Laminack. 2001. *Writing Workshop: Working Through the Hard Parts (and They're All Hard Parts).* Urbana, IL: National Council of Teachers of English.

Rhodes, L., and N. Shanklin. 1993. *Windows into Literacy: Assessing Learners K–8.* Portsmouth, NH: Heinemann.

Roller, C. 1996. *Variability Not Disability: Struggling Readers in a Workshop Classroom.* Newark, DE: International Reading Association.

Romano, T. 1995. *Writing with Passion: Life Stories, Multiple Genres.* Portsmouth, NH: Boynton Cook.

Routman, R. 2004. *Writing Essentials: Raising Expectations and Results While Simplifying Teaching.* Portsmouth, NH: Heinemann.

———. 2003. *Reading Essentials: The Specifics You Need to Teach Reading Well.* Portsmouth, NH: Heinemann.

———. 2000. *Conversations: Strategies for Teaching, Learning, and Evaluating.* Portsmouth, NH: Heinemann.

———. 1991. *Invitations: Changing as Teachers and Learners K–12.* Portsmouth, NH: Heinemann.

Sadler, C. 2001. *Comprehension Strategies for Middle Grade Learners.* Newark, DE: International Reading Association.

Serafini, F. 2004. *Lessons in Comprehension: Explicit Instruction in the Reading Workshop.* Portsmouth, NH: Heinemann.

————. 2001. *The Reading Workshop: Creating Space for Readers.* Portsmouth, NH. Heinemann.

Short, K., J. Harste, and C. Burke. 1996. *Creating Classrooms for Authors and Inquirers.* Portsmouth, NH: Heinemann.

Short, K., J. Schroeder, J. Laird, G. Kauffan, M. Ferguson, and K. M. Crawford. 1996. *Learning Together Through Inquiry: From Columbus to Integrated Curriculum.* Portland, ME: Stenhouse.

Sibberson, F., and K. Szymusiak. 2004. *Bringing Reading to Life: Instruction and Conversation, Grades 3–6* (videotape). Portland, ME: Stenhouse.

————. 2003. *Still Learning to Read: Teaching Students in Grades 3–6.* Portland, ME: Stenhouse.

Snowball, D. 2000. *Focus on Spelling* (videotape). Portland, ME: Stenhouse.

Snowball, D., and F. Bolton. 1999. *Spelling K–8: Planning and Teaching.* Portland, ME: Stenhouse.

Spandel, V. 2000. *Creating Writers Through the 6-Trait Writing, Assessment, and Instruction.* Boston: Allyn and Bacon.

Stead, T. 2004. *Time for Nonfiction* (videotape). Portland, ME: Stenhouse.

————. 2001. *Is That a Fact? Teaching Nonfiction Writing K–3.* Portland, ME: Stenhouse.

Strickland, D., K. Ganske, and J. Monroe. 2002. *Supporting Struggling Readers and Writers: Strategies for Classroom Intervention 3–6.* Portland, ME: Stenhouse.

Szymusiak, K., and F. Sibberson. 2001. *Beyond Leveled Books: Supporting Transitional Readers in Grades 2–5.* Portland, ME: Stenhouse.

Tompkins, G. 1990. *Teaching Writing: Balancing Process and Product.* Columbus, OH: Merrill.

Tovani, C. 2004. *Do I Really Have to Teach Reading? Content Comprehension, Grades 6–12.* Portland, ME: Stenhouse.

————. 2003. *Thoughtful Reading: Teaching Comprehension to Adolescents* (videotape). Portland, ME: Stenhouse.

————. 2000. *I Read It, but I Don't Get It: Comprehension Strategies for Adolescent Readers.* Portland, ME: Stenhouse.

Wilde, S. 2000. *Miscue Analysis Made Easy: Building on Student Strengths.* Portsmouth, NH: Heinemann.

Wilhelm, J. 2001. *Improving Comprehension with Think-Aloud Strategies: Modeling What Good Readers Do.* New York: Scholastic.

Wong-Kam, J., A. Kimura, A. Sumida, J. Ahuna-Ka'ai'ai, and M. Maeshiro. 2001. *Elevating Expectations: A New Take on Accountability, Achievement, and Evaluation.* Portsmouth, NH: Heinemann.

Zwiers, J. 2004. *Building Reading Comprehension Habits in Grades 6–12: A Toolkit of Classroom Activities.* Newark, DE: International Reading Association.

Top 20 Professional Resources

What are the books that I can't live without? What resources do I find myself revisiting throughout the year? Here are my top 20 picks for professional books.

Allington, R. 2000. *What Really Matters for Struggling Readers: Designing Research-Based Programs.* New York: Longman.

Beaver, T. 1998. *The Author's Profile: Assessing Writing in Context.* Portland, ME: Stenhouse.

Brand, M. 2004. *Word Savvy: Integrated Vocabulary, Spelling, and Word Study, Grades 3–6.* Portland, ME: Stenhouse.

Calkins, L. 2000. *The Art of Teaching Reading.* New York: Longman.

———. 1986. *The Art of Teaching Writing.* Portsmouth, NH: Heinemann.

Daniels, H. 2002. *Literature Circles: Voice and Choice in Book Clubs and Reading Groups.* 2nd ed. Portland, ME: Stenhouse.

Fletcher, R. 1993. *What a Writer Needs.* Portsmouth, NH: Heinemann.

Ganske, K. 2000. *Word Journeys: Assessment-Guided Phonics, Spelling, and Vocabulary Instruction.* New York: Guilford Press.

Harvey, S., and A. Goudvis. 2000. *Strategies That Work: Teaching Comprehension to Enhance Understanding.* Portland, ME: Stenhouse.

Heard, G. 2002. *The Revision Toolbox: Teaching Techniques That Work.* Portsmouth, NH: Heinemann.

———. 1999. *Awakening the Heart: Exploring Poetry in the Elementary and Middle School.* Portsmouth, NH: Heinemann.

Hindley, J. 1996. *In the Company of Children.* Portland, ME: Stenhouse.

Keene, E. O., and S. Zimmermann. 1997. *Mosaic of Thought: Teaching Comprehension in a Reader's Workshop.* Portsmouth, NH: Heinemann.

Opitz, M., and T. V. Rasinski. 1998. *Good-Bye Round Robin: 25 Effective Oral Reading Strategies.* Portsmouth, NH: Heinemann.

Ray, K. W. 1999. *Wondrous Words: Writers and Writing in the Elementary Classroom.* Urbana: IL: National Council of Teachers of English.

Strickland, D., K. Ganske, and J. Monroe. 2002. *Supporting Struggling Readers and Writers: Strategies for Classroom Intervention 3–6.* Portland, ME: Stenhouse.

Szymusiak, K., and F. Sibberson. 2001. *Beyond Leveled Books: Supporting Transitional Readers in Grades 2–5.* Portland, ME: Stenhouse.

Tompkins, G. 1990. *Teaching Writing: Balancing Process and Product.* Columbus, OH: Merrill.

Tovani, C. 2000. *I Read It, but I Don't Get It: Comprehension Strategies for Adolescent Readers.* Portland, ME: Stenhouse.

Wilde, S. 2000. *Miscue Analysis Made Easy: Building on Student Strengths.* Portsmouth, NH: Heinemann.

Bibliography

Allen, C. 2001. *The Multigenre Research Paper: Voice, Passion, and Discovery in Grades 4–6*. Portsmouth, NH: Heinemann.

Allington, R. 2000. *What Really Matters to Struggling Readers: Designing Research-Based Programs*. New York: Longman.

Barth, R. 2001. *Learning by Heart*. San Francisco: Jossey-Bass.

Bean, R. M., A. L. Swann, and R. Knaub. 2003. "Reading specialists in schools with exemplary reading programs: Functional, versatile, and prepared." *The Reading Teacher* 56, 446–454.

Beaver, J. M., and M. Carter. 2003. *Developmental Reading Assessment: Grades 4–8*. Parsippany, NJ: Celebration Press.

Beaver, T. 1998. *The Author's Profile: Assessing Writing in Context*. Portland, ME: Stenhouse.

Beers, K. 2002. *When Kids Can't Read, What Teachers Can Do: A Guide for Teachers 6–12*. Portsmouth, NH: Heinemann.

Brand, M. 2004. *Word Savvy: Integrated Vocabulary, Spelling, and Word Study Grades 3–6*. Portland, ME: Stenhouse.

Calkins, L. 2001. *The Art of Teaching Reading*. New York: Longman.

Chandler, K., and the Mapleton Teacher-Research Group. 1999. *Spelling Inquiry: How One Elementary School Caught the Mnemonic Plague*. Portland, ME: Stenhouse.

Cole, A. D. 2002. *Better Answers: Written Performance That Looks Good and Sounds Smart*. Portland, ME: Stenhouse.

Daniels, H. 2002. *Literature Circles: Voice and Choice in Book Clubs and Reading Groups*. 2nd ed. Portland, ME: Stenhouse.

———. 2001. *Looking into Literature Circles* (videotape). Portland, ME: Stenhouse.

Davis, J., and S. Hill. 2003. *The No-Nonsense Guide to Teaching Writing: Strategies, Structures, Solutions*. Portsmouth, NH: Heinemann.

Dillard, A. 1990. *The Writing Life.* New York: HarperCollins.

Dole, J. A. 2004. "The changing role of the reading specialist in school reform." *The Reading Teacher* 57, 462–471.

Dudley-Marling, C., and P. Paugh. 2004. *A Classroom Teacher's Guide to Struggling Readers.* Portsmouth, NH: Heinemann.

Fletcher, R. 1996. *A Writer's Notebook: Unlocking the Writer Within You.* New York: Avon.

———. 1995. *Fig Pudding.* New York: Clarion.

———. 1993. *What a Writer Needs.* Portsmouth, NH: Heinemann.

Fletcher, R., and J. Portalupi. 1998. *Craft Lessons: Teaching Writing K–8.* Portland, ME: Stenhouse.

Fullan, M. 1991. *The New Meaning of Educational Change.* New York: Teacher's College Press.

Ganske, K. 2000. *Word Journeys: Assessment-Guided Phonics, Spelling, and Vocabulary Instruction.* New York: Guilford Press.

Giff, P. R. 2002. *Pictures of Hollis Woods.* New York: Wendy Lamb.

Graves, D. 2001. *The Energy to Teach.* Portsmouth, NH: Heinemann.

Griffith, L., and T. V. Rasinski. 2004. "A focus on fluency: How one teacher incorporated fluency with her reading curriculum." *The Reading Teacher* 58, 126–137.

Guiney, E. 2001. "Coaching isn't just for athletes: The role of teacher leaders." *Phi Delta Kappa* 82 (10), 740–743.

Hannigan, K. 2004. *Ida B . . . and Her Plans to Maximize Fun, Avoid Disaster, and (Possibly) Save the World.* New York: Greenwillow.

Harwayne, S. 1999. *Going Public.* Portsmouth, NH: Heinemann.

Harvey, S., and A. Goudvis. 2003. *Think Nonfiction! Modeling Reading and Research* (videotape). Portland, ME: Stenhouse.

———. 2001. *Strategy Instruction in Action* (videotape). Portland, ME: Stenhouse.

———. 2000. *Strategies That Work: Teaching Comprehension to Enhance Understanding.* Portland, ME: Stenhouse.

Heard, G. 2002. *The Revision Toolbox: Teaching Techniques That Work.* Portsmouth, NH: Heinemann.

Hindley, J. 1996. *In the Company of Children.* Portland, ME: Stenhouse.

Hudson, R., H. Lane, and P. Pullen. 2005. "Reading fluency assessment and instruction: What why and how?" *The Reading Teacher* 58, 702–714.

Independent Review Panel. 2001. *Improving the Odds: A Report on Title I from the Independent Review Panel.* Christopher Cross, Chairman, Independent Review Panel.

Kohn, A. 2004. *What Does It Mean to Be Well-Educated? And Other Essays on Standards, Grading, and Other Follies.* New York: Beacon Press.

Krashen, S. 2004. *The Power of Reading: Insights from the Research.* Portsmouth, NH: Heinnemann.

Lane, B. 1993. *After the End: Teaching and Learning Creative Revision.* Portsmouth, NH: Heinemann.

Lyons, C. A., and G. S. Pinnell. 2001. *Systems for Change in Literacy Education: A Guide to Professional Development.* Portsmouth, NH: Heinemann.